GOOD APPLE AND MATH FUN

BY
JERRY ATEN

ILLUSTRATED BY VANESSA FILKINS

Cover by Kathryn Hyndman

Copyright © Good Apple, Inc., 1990 Revised

ISBN No. 0-86653-023-1

Printing No. 98765

Good Apple, Inc.
1204 Buchanan St., Box 299
Carthage, IL 62321

TABLE OF CONTENTS

GA279

GA279

GA279

A MESSAGE TO THE READER

The whole purpose of this book is to provide students with a variety of learning options that will enrich the core of basic instruction they have already received. The main focus of these projects and activities lies within the learning center. There are learning center ideas presented throughout the book that are offered as suggestions because they have a proven track record in the classroom. Obviously, space and available resources will play the most important roles in determining the specific type of learning center you create.

When it comes to the management of a classroom using the learning center approach, there must be some very positive and definite well-made plans on the part of the teacher. The planning and record-keeping must be organized so as to provide for almost total individualization on the part of the students and to require minimum intervention on the part of the teacher.

To determine the types of activities and projects that will be stationed in the learning center, the teacher must first assess just what it is that he/she hopes to accomplish there. Is he/she really providing for a variety of ability levels? Are the tasks laid out really appropriate to the material presented to the class? Will those tasks that are assigned provide for a meaningful learning experience . . . or are they merely "busy work"?

Since many students may not be familiar with this type of learning environment, it is appropriate to spend some time with them explaining fully just what is expected of them and the types of behaviors that will not be tolerated.

A simple behavior agreement similar to the one found in this book can go a long way toward making a child realize the responsibilities he/she is assuming. The trick is to keep it simple to avoid confusion, but also to be very specific about what it is that you want children to do.

Learning Can Be Fun!

GA279

Once the children recognize the behavioral commitment they have made, it is time to lay before them the various options they have available and to get a commitment from them as to those specific tasks which they will choose to complete. Perhaps the best way to accomplish this is through an actual contractual arrangement with the student. There is an example of such a contract in this book as well as some helpful hints on how to handle contract work with students. The bottom line here is for the teacher to insist that children live up to the commitments they have made.

There are bulletin board ideas scattered throughout as well as a number of learning center suggestions. In addition, there are educational games and seatwork type activities (both for the individual and for small groups). There are also pages which contain four independent task cards each. To gain full benefit from the use of these cards, it is a good idea to cut them apart and laminate or cover them with Con-Tact paper to ensure their durability. It is also advisable to cover the game boards in the same manner. Finally, there are activities that involve students in real life problematic simulations (Main Street Math) to demonstrate the importance of mathematics in everyday life.

That was really the main purpose of this book. To be able to motivate kids to appreciate just how important mathematics is and will continue to be to them was the whole idea. If they have a little fun along the way. . . so much the better!

A WORD ABOUT LEARNING CENTERS

The whole idea of a learning center is not to replace the classroom teacher, but to move children away from teacher-centered direction toward more independent study. Having a variety of materials, activities and projects also allows the student the opportunity to choose something he/she wants to do rather than something the teacher has directed be done.

Learning centers help to provide for the individual differences in children. Each child runs on a different track, and if we are going to get the very best from children, then we must provide them with learning activities that motivate them and cater to their needs. Pity the teacher who fails to recognize these differences in the needs of her children.

Another advantage in using the learning center approach is the ability to create a variety of study environments. While some projects and activities can be designed for individuals, others should be adapted to small group work. It is also advisable to have the entire class participate in certain projects. The interaction from such group involvement will vary, but there should be something for everyone when different arrangements are created for different students.

GA279

The materials you place in your learning centers should also be durable. Except for the consumable activity sheets, all other projects and activities should either be laminated or covered with Con-Tact paper to ensure their durability. It's a good idea to use tagboard or heavy paper to add further life to the materials you choose. Remember that several children are going to handle them over a period of time.

Each center you make should be pretty much self-contained. The less moving about students have to do, the more they are going to become involved in the project at hand. Either a long or round table usually works best. If you don't have one available, another alternative is to use a bookcase. Some schools have movable panels or study carrels, which can help to create the proper environment for learning center work. Be certain to include enough chairs so that each child has a place to sit. Do not overcrowd your center. Too many children in the same area trying to work on the same project will only get in one another's way; this can also provide them with an opportunity to waste time.

To solve this problem of overcrowding, it is suggested that the teacher enter into a contract with each student, with the student and teacher agreeing on just what should be done as well as when it should be done.

CONTRACTS FOR KIDS

1. Each student should fully understand the terms of the contract.

2. Encourage the students to be realistic about their goals. They should be left with the idea that each student should choose only what he/she really thinks he/she can achieve. Oftentimes children get caught up in arrangements which in reality they have little chance of completing. Their purpose in doing so is usually to gain the favor of the teacher.

3. The reward for completing the contract should come soon after the student has completed the terms of the agreement.

4. The philosophy behind contracting lies in encouraging greater responsibility on the part of the student. Offer as much help as needed when children are first learning this concept. Some children may not have been involved in this type of commitment before.

5. Rewards should only be given to those who actually live up to the terms of their contracts. To those who try very hard but do not quite get there, it's "better luck next time." You can offer them encouragement for the future, but they should not be rewarded, as this places some questions in the minds of those students who actually complete their contracts about the importance of fulfillment.

6. Use language in contracts that can be clearly understood by students.

GA279

KID CONTRACT

Be it hereby established that _____
                                              (name of student)

will successfully complete _____

_____
                          (specific tasks to be completed)

during the time period determined as _____

_____
                          (date when contract must be fulfilled)

Be it further stated that upon completion of the above conditions, the teacher _____

_____
                                        (name of teacher)

will compensate said student with the following reward:

_____

_____

_____
                                        (explanation of reward)

Date of Contract:_____

Signature: _____
                                        student

_____
                                        teacher

GA279

STUDENT BEHAVIOR AGREEMENT

As a follow-up, the student's *very first step* toward this independence should be a commitment similar to the one below in which the student actually promises to conform to acceptable school behavior. The written commitment seems to encourage much more appropriate behavior.

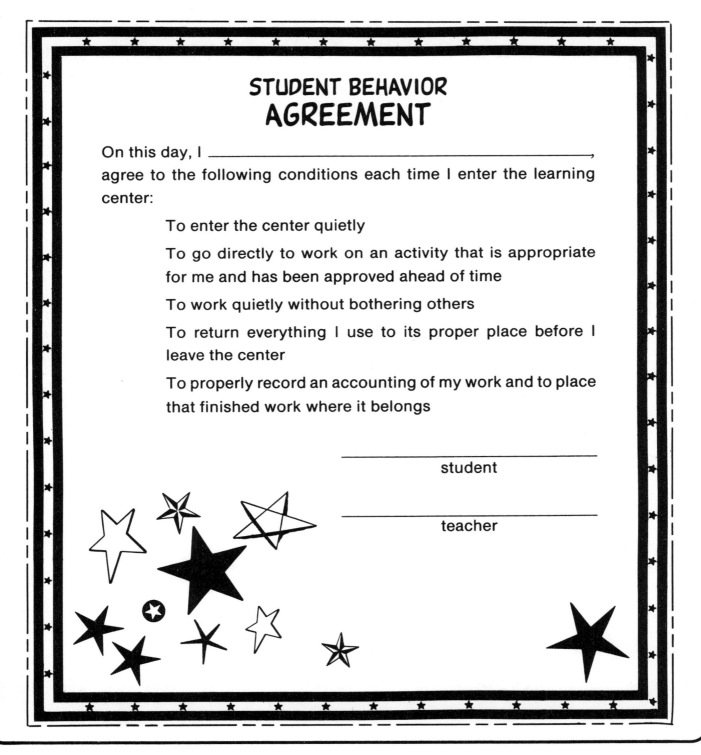

STUDENT BEHAVIOR AGREEMENT

On this day, I _____
agree to the following conditions each time I enter the learning center:

To enter the center quietly

To go directly to work on an activity that is appropriate for me and has been approved ahead of time

To work quietly without bothering others

To return everything I use to its proper place before I leave the center

To properly record an accounting of my work and to place that finished work where it belongs

_____
student

_____
teacher

GA279

PLACE VALUE CENTER

Prepare seven different worksheets using examples that are similar to those found on these two pages. You should include enough problems similar to those below and on the next page to fill up an entire activity sheet. Then you can reproduce them and place several copies of each in separate folders. Clip an answer key to the back of each folder to allow student self checking. Place the manila folders either inside a larger box or tack the folders to a bulletin board within the center.

Try to place the center near a bulletin board area where you can create a display that will motivate and encourage your students to participate in a center's activities.

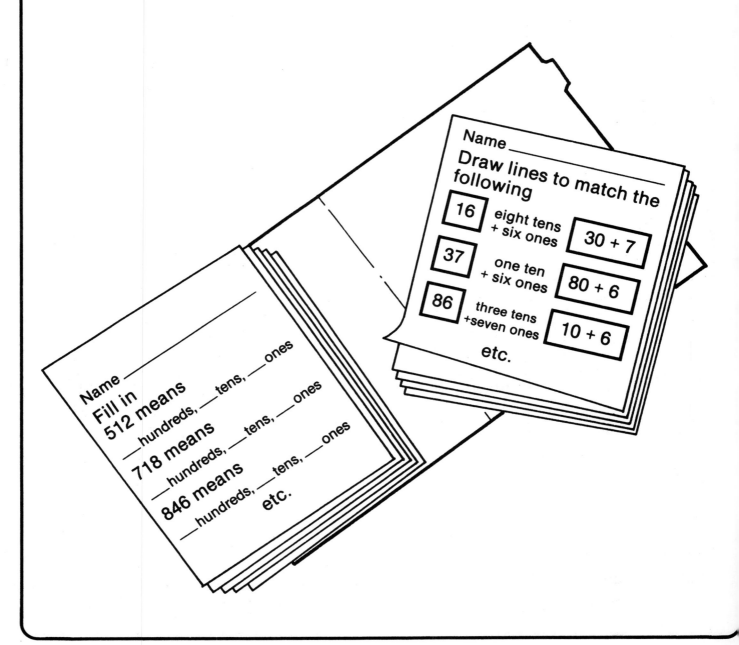

Name _____
Draw lines to match the following

16   eight tens + six ones   30 + 7

37   one ten + six ones   80 + 6

86   three tens + seven ones   10 + 6

etc.

Name _____
Fill in
512 means ____ hundreds, ____ tens, ____ ones
718 means ____ hundreds, ____ tens, ____ ones
846 means ____ hundreds, ____ tens, ____ ones
etc.

GA27

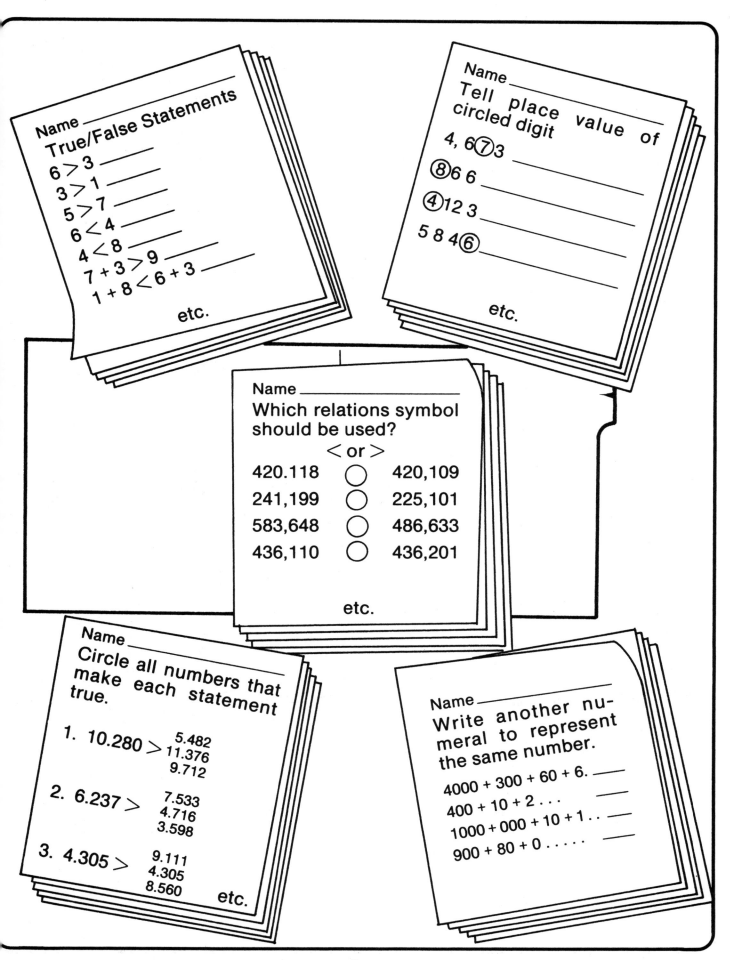

Name _____
True/False Statements
6 > 3 _____
3 > 1 _____
5 > 7 _____
6 < 4 _____
4 < 8 _____
7 + 3 > 9 _____
1 + 8 < 6 + 3 _____
etc.

Name _____
Tell place value of circled digit
4, 6⑦3 _____
⑧6 6 _____
④12 3 _____
5 8 4⑥ _____
etc.

Name _____
Which relations symbol should be used?
< or >
420.118 ◯ 420,109
241,199 ◯ 225,101
583,648 ◯ 486,633
436,110 ◯ 436,201
etc.

Name _____
Circle all numbers that make each statement true.
1. 10.280 > 5.482
             11.376
             9.712

2. 6.237 > 7.533
            4.716
            3.598

3. 4.305 > 9.111
            4.305
            8.560
etc.

Name _____
Write another numeral to represent the same number.
4000 + 300 + 60 + 6. ___
400 + 10 + 2 . . . ___
1000 + 000 + 10 + 1 . . ___
900 + 80 + 0 . . . . . ___

GA279

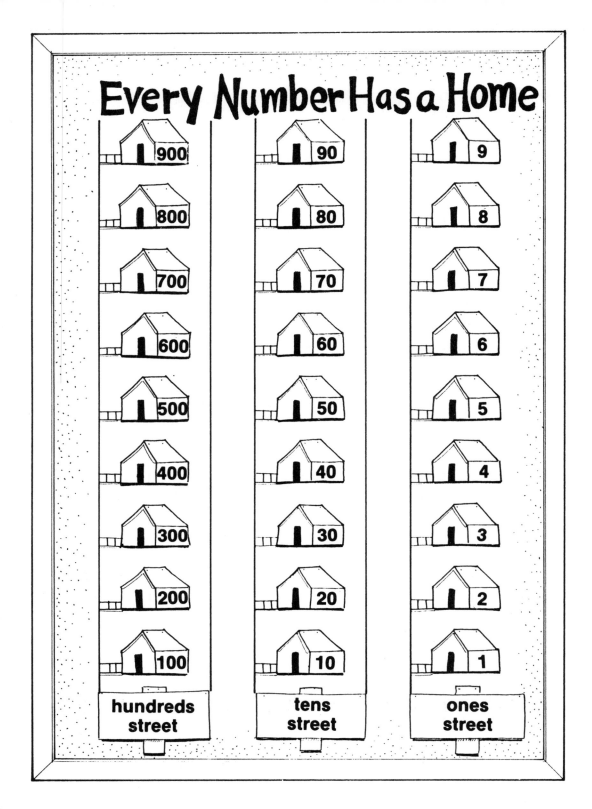

Every Number Has a Home

Use poster board for background and cut houses out of various colors of construction paper. Use black felt-tipped marker to label numbers and street signs. Place the bulletin board in the Place Value Learning Center to capture student attention.

On the first day the board is placed in the learning center, ask students if they understand the concept behind the idea. If they do not, explain to them thoroughly.

10

GA279

IT'S "EVEN" A-MAZING

Find your way through this maze of odd numbers by tracing the route taken by the *evens* from the start to the finish.

START 2	4	17	39	49
59	33	12	89	1
91	18	73	57	9
36	42	50	31	13
51	37	82	23	29
7	19	40	92	14
37	43	87	56	98
25	3	67	47	68 FINISH

GA279

. . . AND WHEN IN ROME

You may think you will never have any use for Roman numerals. Just wait! Look at the cornerstone of any old building. Do you see some Roman numerals? If not, you may have to walk all the way around the building, but they should be there someplace. Those numbers represent the year in which the building was built; and unless you know about Roman numerals, you'll just never really know that important fact, will you?

Here are some of the numerals used by the ancient Romans:

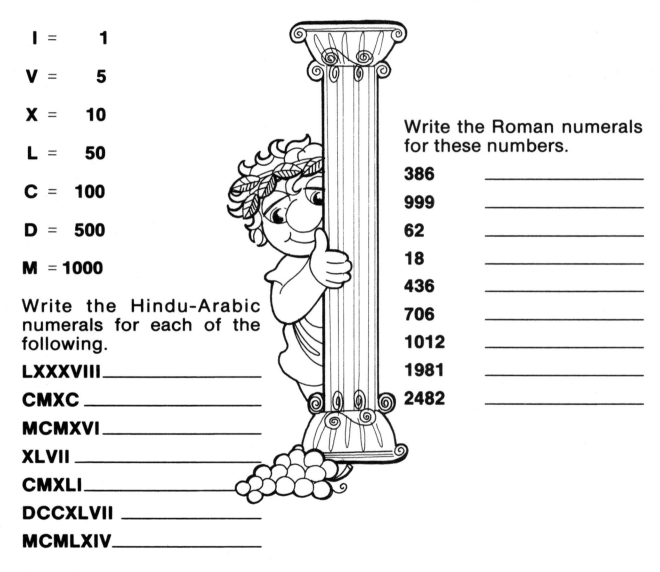

I = 1

V = 5

X = 10

L = 50

C = 100

D = 500

M = 1000

Write the Hindu-Arabic numerals for each of the following.

LXXXVIII_____

CMXC _____

MCMXVI_____

XLVII _____

CMXLI_____

DCCXLVII _____

MCMLXIV_____

Write the Roman numerals for these numbers.

386 _____

999 _____

62 _____

18 _____

436 _____

706 _____

1012 _____

1981 _____

2482 _____

See! There's one reason already for knowing how to read Roman numerals. Another reason is to try to dazzle your math teacher with your brilliance. She may not know how really smart you are! Can you think of any more reasons?

GA279

HIDDEN ANIMAL

Find the hidden animal in the puzzle below by coloring in all even-numbered areas. Leave the odd-numbered areas alone.

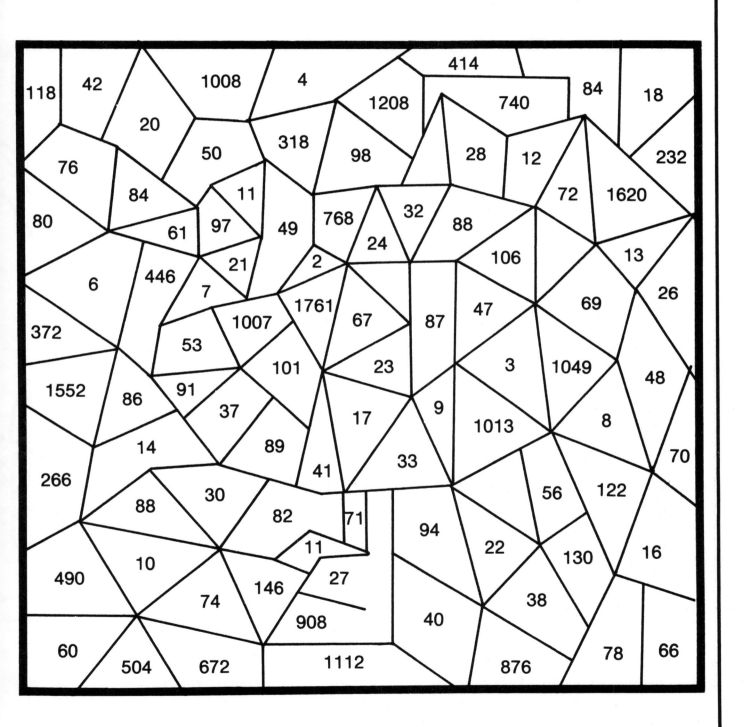

GA279

Mrs. Jackson keeps records for the Pink Pony Cafe. A part of her job involves recording the number of lunches that are served annually in the cafe. Last year she reported that forty-one thousand, eight hundred seventy-six lunches were served. Write this number.

_____

Two years ago the restaurant served forty-two thousand, two hundred three lunches. Write down the number that represents this many lunches. Then compare the number of lunches served two years ago with the number served last year. Was the number greater than (>) or less than (<)?

_____

Other figures which she recorded of importance: Last year the Pink Pony served thirty-two thousand, seven hundred eighteen cups of coffee. Two years ago it served thirty thousand, nine hundred sixty-nine. Write both of these numbers. _____

_____

Two years ago the cafe sold five thousand, two hundred thirty-two cartons of milk. Last year only four thousand, eight hundred forty-eight were sold. Compare these two numbers by writing both, then telling in which year more cartons of milk were sold.

_____

_____

GA279

Last year the Pink Pony recorded sales of four thousand, six hundred fifteen glasses of iced tea, while sales of two years ago amounted to four thousand, eight hundred sixteen. Write down both of these figures. In which year were people thirstier for iced tea? _____

Mrs. Jackson also found that two years ago three thousand, eight-hundred twenty-six soft drinks were served during lunch, whereas last year there were four thousand, eighty-eight soft drinks served. Write down both of these figures. _____

_____

Set up a table using the symbols (>) for greater than and (<) for less than to show how the two years compare. From all this information, which year looks like the better year for the Pink Pony Cafe?

Why do you suppose anyone would care about any of the information Mrs. Jackson has recorded? Of what use is it? Who would really want to know? What use can be made of this data?

IN PROPER SEQUENCE

See if you can read the thoughts on Becky's mind in the game below . . .

When Tom says:

3
9
18
36

Becky says:

6
12
21
39

It shouldn't take you long to figure out that Becky is adding 3 every time Tom says a number . . . right???

Place yourself now in Becky's shoes and fill in the missing numbers below.

6	8	___	12	___	16	___	___
1	6	11	___	21	___	___	36
16	14	15	___	14	12	___	___
36	32	___	24	___	16	___	8
0	1	3	6	___	___	___	___
___	___	36	___	___	___	___	86
1	1	2	6	___	___	___	___
0	6	8	4	___	___	8	___

GA279

A SEQUENCE I KNOW

Design a puzzle of your own and try to stump your classmates.

_____ — _____ — _____ — _____ — _____ — _____

_____ — _____ — _____ — _____ — _____ — _____

_____ — _____ — _____ — _____ — _____ — _____

_____ — _____ — _____ — _____ — _____ — _____

_____ — _____ — _____ — _____ — _____ — _____ — _____

_____ — _____ — _____ — _____ — _____ — _____

_____ — _____ — _____ — _____ — _____ — _____

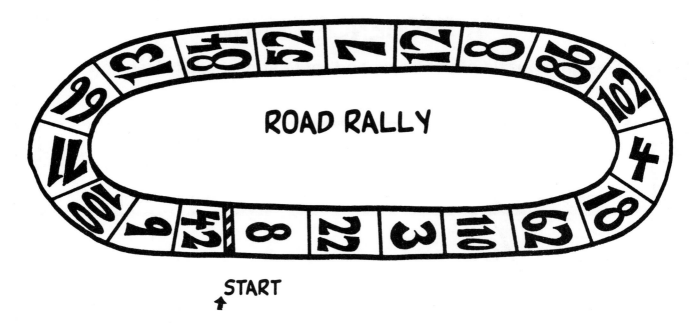

ROAD RALLY

START

Gameboard is constructed on 14" x 14" tagboard. Laminate or cover with Con-Tact paper.

Either two or three players can play this game. Each player has a token and a scorecard similar to the one on this page.

The first player rolls the die and advances his/her token the number of spaces indicated on the die. He/She then records on the score sheet the place value of the number where the token landed. The second player then rolls the die and advances accordingly. Each player rolls the die six times. At the end of six rounds, players then total up the number of ones, tens and hundreds each has. That total is then written as a whole number and the player with the largest number wins.

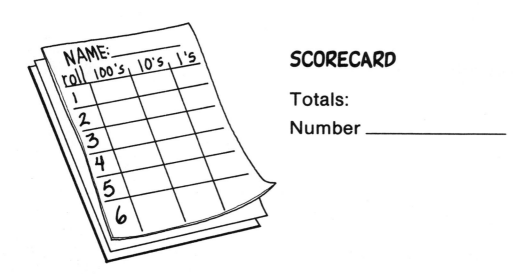

SCORECARD

Totals:

Number _____

18

Has Earned a Place at the Head of the Class for Work in Place Value

_____
teacher

_____
student

HAS SCORED A HIT IN MATH

_____
teacher

GA279

The number of miles can be changed to suit the level of student.

SAMPLE PROBLEM
What is the distance from A to D? To get the correct answer, the student would have to add the following:

  5 . . . the distance of A to B
 53 . . . the distance of B to C
217 . . . the distance of C to D

SAMPLE PROBLEM
What is the distance from E to H? To get the correct answer, the student would have to add the following:

310 . . . the distance of E to F
 62 . . . the distance of F to G
 15 . . . the distance of G to H

GA279

DEEP SEA SUBTRACTION

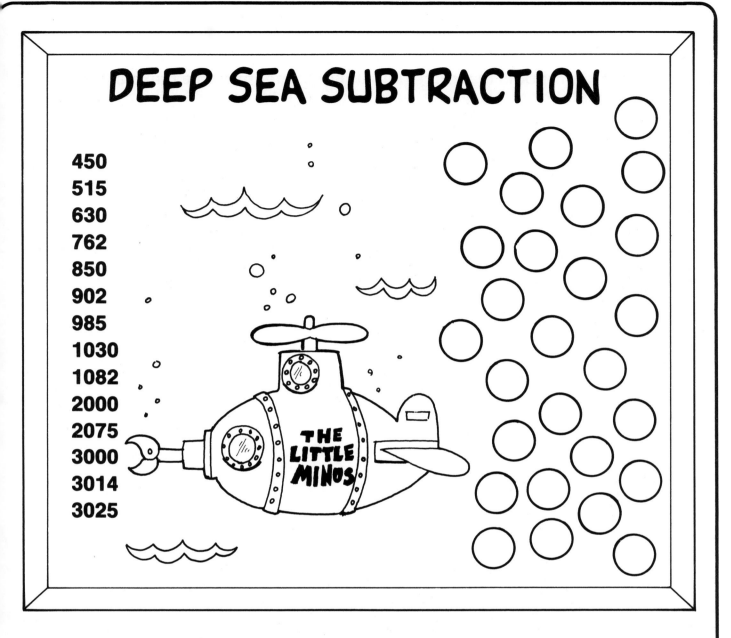

450
515
630
762
850
902
985
1030
1082
2000
2075
3000
3014
3025

THE LITTLE MINUS

Here is a bulletin board idea for the whole class. Use light blue construction paper, poster board or cloth for the background in this deep sea delight. Make the LITTLE MINUS out of a contrasting color of poster board and laminate to ensure durability. The numbers on the depth chart, the letters and the forty bubbles are similarly made using a contrasting color that can easily be seen.

The reverse side of each bubble has a number on it that is smaller than any of the numbers on the depth chart. Have one of your students move the LITTLE MINUS to any depth desired. He/She then chooses one of the bubbles to serve as the subtrahend. The student then subtracts the number on the bubble from the depth of the LITTLE MINUS—with the rest of the class checking for accuracy. Then it's someone else's turn.

SPOOL CENTER

Old wooden spools that once held utility company cable make excellent learning stations. They can be painted bright colors to liven up your learning center even more. Use dividers in the center to provide for individual learning stations. The best thing about this type of center is that it doesn't cost anything. Local utility companies are usually more than happy to donate the spools to the schools.

There are several different types of learning centers that can be used with a subject like mathematics. Scattered throughout this book are several suggestions for the construction and design of learning centers. The reader will be able to adapt each to other specific content areas. Not to be forgotten are the all-important factors of space limitations and the availability of materials. Design and arrangement should not be limited to any one specific type of classroom. Learning centers are effective educational tools in both traditional and open space classrooms. It usually comes down to a case of teacher ingenuity in determining the best possible use of the available space and resources.

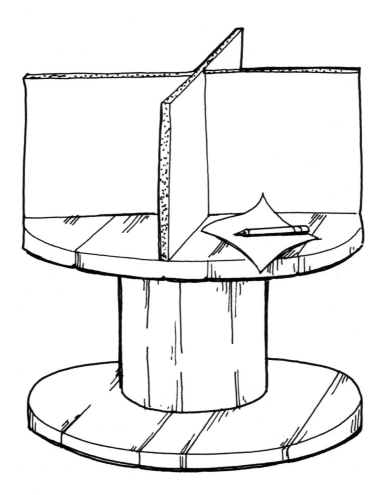

GA279

COVER 20

Using tagboard, construct boards for this game similar to the one shown below. To preserve the life of the game boards, laminate each board. You will also need to make several boards, as each player needs a board.

Students will need four dice to play this game plus at least twenty tokens per player. The object of the game is to cover all twenty numbers with tokens.

Players roll a single die to determine order of play. The highest roll goes first. The first player rolls the dice, then adds the spots on the dice. Once he/she has that sum, he/she covers the same number on the game board with a token and passes the dice on to the next player. Should a roll produce a combination that is already covered, play merely moves on to the next player.

Players *always* have the option of deciding *how many* dice to use prior to each roll. A player can choose to roll a single die, a combination of two dice, a combination of three dice, or a combined total of all four dice. The numbers covered on his/her board will more than likely determine the number of dice used. The first player to cover all twenty of the numbers on his/her board is the winner of the game.

GA279

GOOD . . . BETTER . . . BEST

Which of the following is a *good* buy?

Last week lettuce sold for $.89/head. This week lettuce is on sale for $.69/head. Is lettuce a good buy this week?

Should the wise shopper stock up on lettuce when the price is low? Is it wise to buy three heads of lettuce? How about five heads? Ten heads? What is wrong with this type of thinking?

Last week peanut butter (a top brand name) sold for $2.39 for a 64-oz. jar. This week that same jar of peanut butter costs $2.79. Is peanut butter a good buy this week? What could possibly cause the price to rise so sharply in just seven days?

What things must be considered when deciding whether or not to buy the peanut butter at this high price?

Is it best to buy . . . .

. . . a 32-oz. bottle of fabric softener for $2.09?

. . . a 64-oz. bottle of fabric softener for $3.84?

. . .or a 96-oz. bottle of fabric softener for $5.19?

GA279

Which is the *best* buy?

A small 12-inch pizza for $5.95?

A medium sized 14-inch pizza for $7.19?

A large sized pizza with a diameter of 16 inches for $8.19?

How are you going to possibly calculate which of the above is the best buy?

Which is the *best* buy?

. . .an 11-oz. box of breakfast food for $1.49?

. . .a 13-oz. box of the same breakfast food for $1.79?

. . .or a one-pound box (16 oz.) of breakfast food for $1.99?

Which is the *better* buy?

one cassette for $8.95 or two cassettes for $14.95?

six breakfast rolls for $.89 or a dozen for $1.80?

two ties for $12.00 or three ties for $16.00?

three golf balls for $6.00 or one dozen of the same balls for $22.00?

one head of lettuce for $.69 or three heads for $1.77?

four colored pens for $.99 or a package of six pens for $1.59?

What considerations other than just price should be made when buying any of the above?

GA279

MAKING CHANGE

If you were a clerk in a department store and the following purchases were made by people who passed through "your register," how much change would you give to each of them?

After you've calculated the amount of change the customers have coming, draw in the denominations you would give to them and make the drawings in the order in which you would hand the change to the customers.

For example, a purchase that costs $.79 has $.04 tax added on for a total of $.83. If the buyer gives you a dollar bill, you owe the customer $.17. To make change properly, you should give the customer two pennies, one nickel and one dime as shown.

Figure the change on these purchases and draw pictures of the money that should be given back.

A lady's bill comes to $5.95 plus she owes $.30 tax. She gives you two five-dollar bills.

The bill for a tennis racket comes to $23.00. There is also $1.15 owed in tax. The buyer gives you a twenty-dollar bill and a ten-dollar bill.

GA279

The next customer through your aisle has purchases totaling $37.87 (including tax). You are given a fifty-dollar bill.

A person buys a vaporizer for $14.00. Tax comes to $.70 and the buyer gives you a twenty-dollar bill.

The bill on a number of small items totals $16.20. If sales tax amounts to $.81 and the buyer gives you a twenty-dollar bill, figure the change she has coming back.

Your final customer is the "big spender" of the day and has purchases that total $86.79. She gives you a one hundred-dollar bill. Calculate the change you should return to this customer.

GA279

NUMBER WORMS

FILL IN MISSING SYMBOLS BELOW.

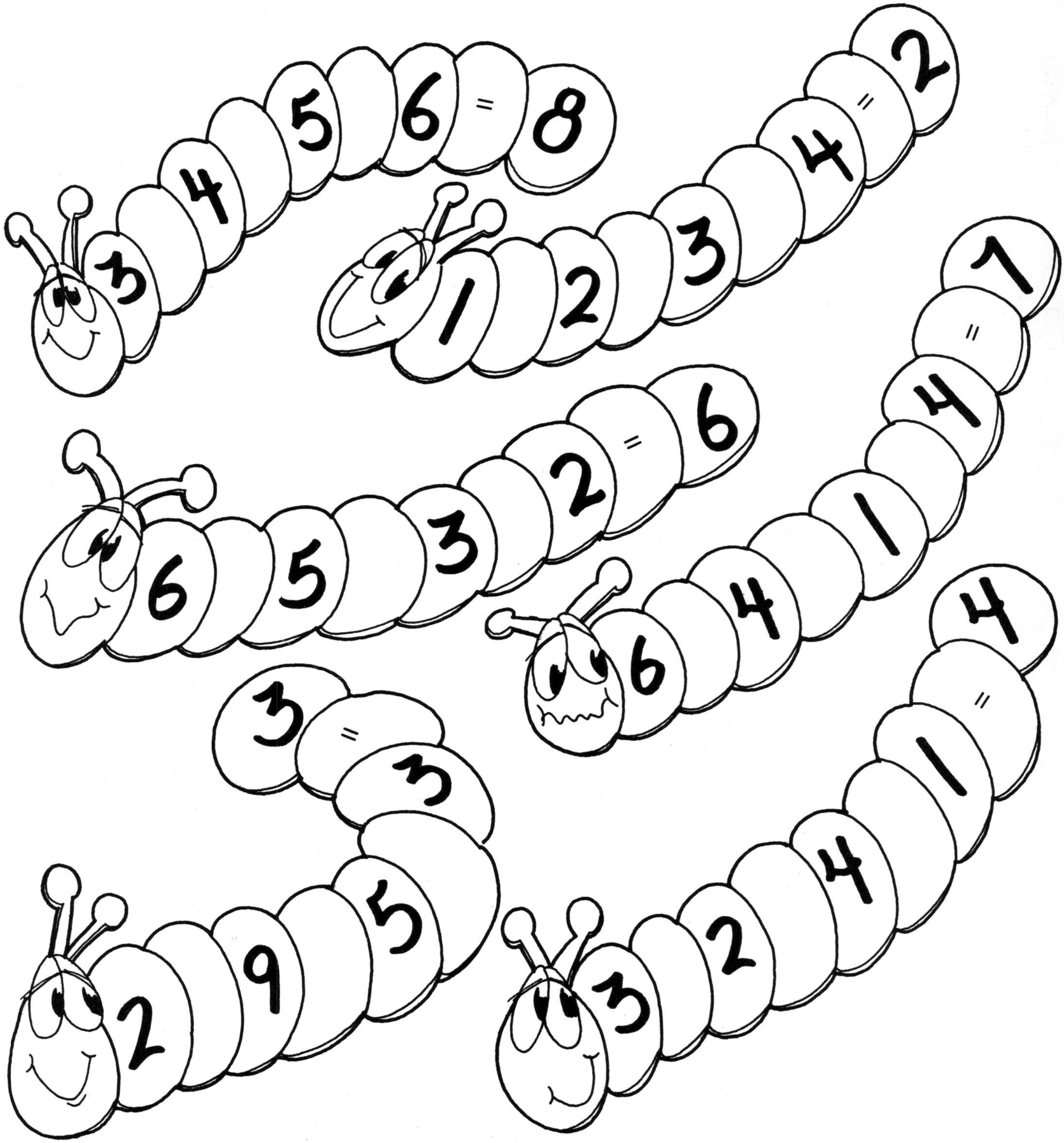

Worm 1: 3 4 5 6 = 8

Worm 2: 1 2 3 4 = 2

Worm 3: 6 5 3 2 = 6

Worm 4: 6 4 1 4 = 1

Worm 5: 3 = 3

Worm 6: 2 9 5

Worm 7: 3 2 4 1 = 4

28

SUBTRACTO

Construct game cards similar to the card shown below. Make several cards, all containing the same numbers; however, numbers should be placed in different places on each card. You can also make many other combinations by changing *minuends* and *subtrahends*. Laminate or cover each with Con-Tact paper to ensure durability. Players will also need several tokens.

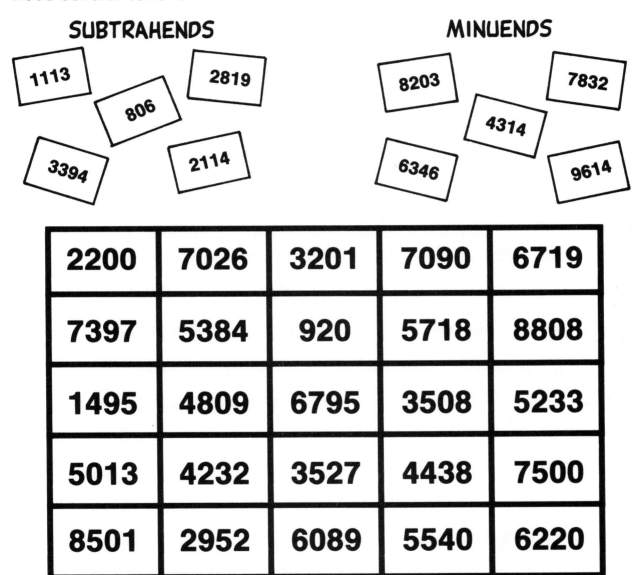

SUBTRAHENDS

1113   806   2819   3394   2114

MINUENDS

8203   4314   7832   6346   9614

2200	7026	3201	7090	6719
7397	5384	920	5718	8808
1495	4809	6795	3508	5233
5013	4232	3527	4438	7500
8501	2952	6089	5540	6220

This game is played by two players. Each player selects a game card. The first player selects a number from the pool of *minuends* and a number from the pool of *subtrahends*. He/She then subtracts and places a token on the difference.

The second player also places a token that covers the number wherever it may appear on his/her game card. The first player to complete a row vertically, horizontally or diagonally wins.

GA279

HIGH ROLLER

Two rollers can play this game. Both players roll the dice to see who goes first. Both players roll both dice and then add the two together to get the total.

Both players start at zero. The idea of the game is to score *exactly* 50 points. Each player has the choice of either adding or subtracting the roll from his/her score. If a player's total at any given moment will exceed 50, then there is no choice . . . . he/she must subtract the roll from his/her total.

For example, Player A has accumulated a total of 43 points from previous rolls. He/She then rolls a 5 and a 4 on the next roll. Adding the two together would give 9 plus the original 43 or a total of 52 points (which is beyond 50). Thus there would be no choice but to subtract the roll (9) from his/her score which would leave a net score of 34. He/She must try again when it is his/her turn. To win the game, a player must land exactly on the accumulated total of 50. Keep all rolls and totals on a score sheet to check the final outcome.

score sheet

Dee	Tim
6	7
4	3
10	12
7	10
12	3
2	8
TOTAL	TOTAL

43 + 9 or 43 – 9?

GA279

LET THE SUM SHINE IN

Add all the numbers on the rays together to get a really brightly shining sum.

GA279

SUPERSHOPPING FOR GROCERIES

You'll need to team up with a friend for this one. You and your friend are going to actually go to some grocery stores and see what certain food items cost these days. It's really pretty wise shopping to compare prices at different stores every once in awhile. After all, these days you want to stretch those dollars just as far as they will go. Parents do this all the time. Let's have you give them some help. First, look closely at the list below.

1-lb. pkg. Parkay margarine
12-oz. can Minute Maid frozen orange juice
5-lb. bag Gold Medal flour
1-lb. box Nabisco Premium Saltines
5-lb. bag C & H sugar
3 lb. tin Crisco shortening
1-lb. pkg. Oscar Mayer bacon
4-oz. can Pennsylvania Dutchman mushrooms
6½ oz. can Chicken of the Sea tuna
46 oz. can Hi-C orange drink
12-shell box Ortega taco shells

If you are going to really *compare* as we are doing in this little mission, then you are going to have to look very closely in each case at both the *quantity* and the *brand name*.

Armed with the list and a sheet of scratch paper, you and your pal should go to at least two *different* stores. Find every item on the list in each store and record its *exact* cost. You might even take along a parent or older brother/sister to help. Once you've completed all the "leg work," sit down with your friend and figure out which store has the "best buys" according to the items you have on your list.

GA279

How do things like convenience, location, service and cleanliness enter into a mom's or dad's decision to buy the family groceries at a certain place?

Perhaps you've heard someone say, "You're just paying for the name when you buy . . . ." Sometimes brand name isn't really very important to people when they buy their groceries. There are even groceries today that are packaged in containers without any brand name on them at all. They're called *generic* foods and they really do save you $$$$.

The quality of *generic* foods may be just as high as some of the brand names or it may not. It's just a matter of personal taste. One thing for certain, though, is that no money is spent on advertising (which adds to the cost of the groceries we buy).

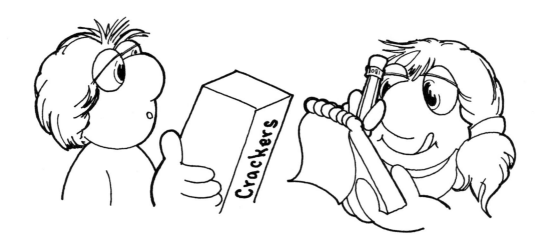

With your friend, go back to those same two stores (or choose two others if you like) and this time find the *least expensive* package or container that holds the same quantity as the package on your list.

Now which store offers the *better* buys? Compare the lists item for item. Then total them all up. When you get home, ask one of your parents whether *brand name* or *price* is more important at your house.

There's a neat word for all this "research" you've been doing. It's called *consumerism*.

GA279

OSCAR N. OCTOPUS

Fill in the missing numbers on Oscar's tentacles. The number on the end of each tentacle is the sum of the addends on that tentacle including the number in the center.

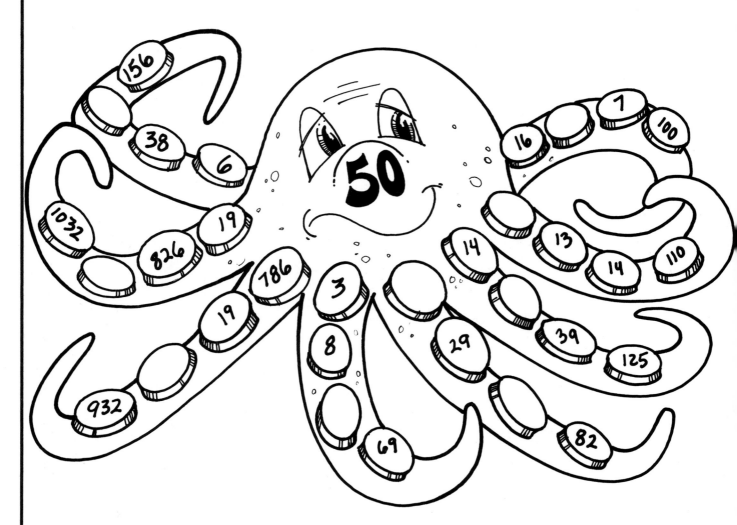

What is the total sum of all the missing numbers?

34

GA279

MORE NUMBER WORMS

Fill in the missing numbers to complete these number worms.

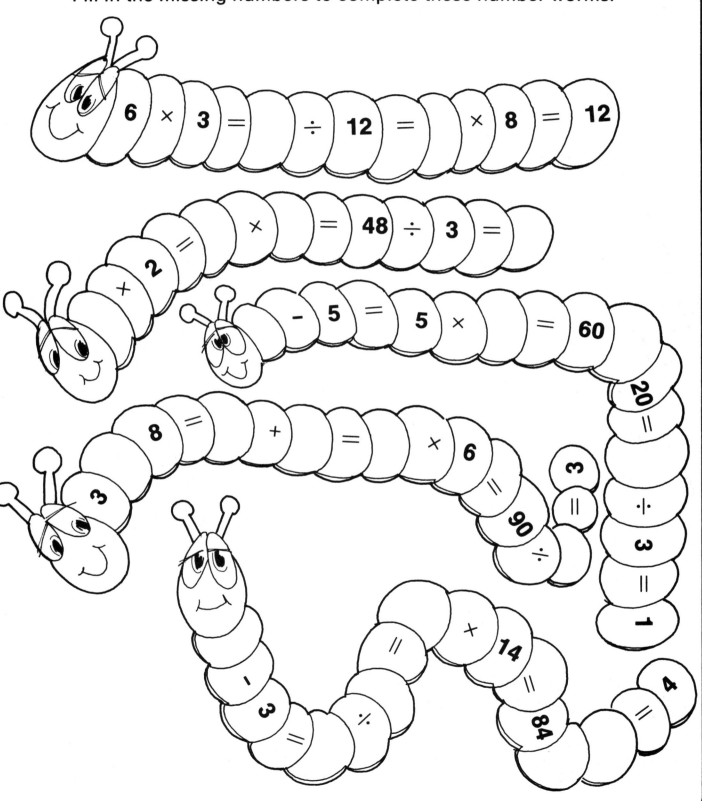

GA279

SHUTTER BUG

Wendy's dad has decided to buy a 35 mm camera for next summer's family vacation. After much "research" reading photography magazines and books, listening to the advice of friends who already own 35 mm cameras and catching the many "great failures" of the different cameras advertised on TV, Wendy's dad has decided on the camera he feels is best for his family. His main decision rested on buying an outfit that he could conveniently add to later on as he learned how to take better pictures.

Once the choice of *which* camera was made, the next step was to decide just *where to buy* the outfit. There are several camera stores in Wendy's town, so she and her dad spent one Saturday morning checking them all out. The prices were pretty much the same and all stores seemed to offer the "very best of service." Below are the quoted prices in each of the three stores visited.

Monty's Cameraland

camera body. . .$289.95; additional charge for f1.4 lens. . .$45.00; f111 electronic flash attachment . . .$48.95; action case $20.00; AZ–1 telephoto lens. . .$109.95; ultraviolet filter. . . $8.95.

Camera King

camera body. . .$279.95; additional charge for f1.4 lens. . .$42; f111 electronic flash attachment. . .$45.95; action case. . .$18.95; AZ–1 telephoto lens. . .$113.95; an ultraviolet filter. . . $5.95.

The Zoom Zone

. . .offered this weekend package special which included the camera body, the f1.4 lens and the action case for $339.95. The f111 electronic flash attachment sells for $49.95 and the AZ–1 telephoto lens for $110.00. The salesman offered to "throw in" the ultraviolet filter.

Calculate the total cost for each of these camera "deals." Be sure to also add on 5 percent for sales tax.

GA279

Wendy and her dad then went home to figure out the "best deal." They were looking through one of the photography magazines and came across the advertisement below from the 41st Street Photo.

Camera body. . .$249.95; extra charge for the f1.4 lens. . .$40; AZ-1 telephoto lens. . .$105.00; action case. . .$20; f111 electronic flash attachment. . .$39.95; ultraviolet filter. . .$5.95.

To find out more, Wendy's dad called a toll free 800 number. He was told that there would also be the added advantage of not having to pay the 5% sales tax they would have to pay if they bought in town. There would, however, be insurance costs of $7.50 plus $3.50 for shipping "action express" (air) and $2.00 more for processing the order.

Aside from price, what other considerations should she and her dad make before buying?

What are the advantages of buying "in town"?

What are the disadvantages in this case?

What advantages does the mail order idea offer?

What are its disadvantages?

Considering all of the above information, what choice should Wendy and her dad make in buying a camera?

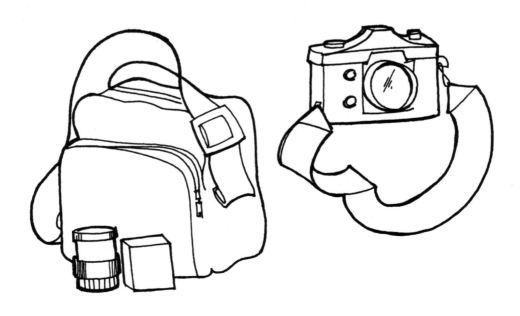

GA279

X-OUT

To play this game you will need some graph paper that is cut into squares containing 100 of the smaller squares each (10 x 10). Each player will need one of these sheets to use as a game board as well as a felt-tipped marking pen and a pair of dice.

To begin, players all roll the dice to determine order of play (with high roll going first). Player A then rolls the dice. He/She adds the two together and crosses out the same number of spaces as in the combined total of the dice roll. Other players must mentally do the same to "check the opposition." The first player to cross out all of his/her boxes wins. Near the end of the game players must roll the *exact* number of spaces remaining in order to play.

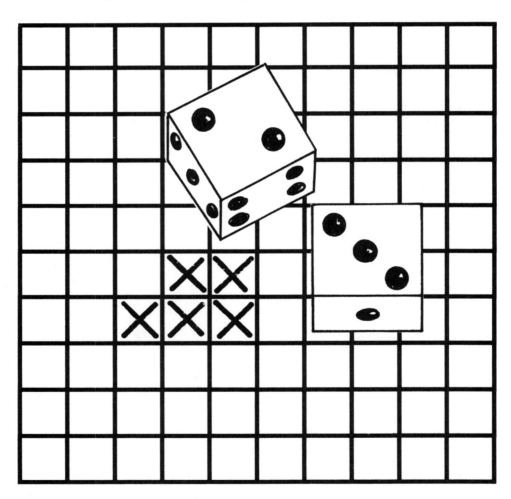

If, for example, Player A rolls a two and three as shown, he/she would cross out five boxes on his/her game board. Near the end of the game, he/she may have four spaces left blank. To win, that player would have to roll exactly a four. Any other roll would not permit him/her to play and the dice would advance to the next player.

GA279

CROSSING PATHS

Construct a game board similar to the one below. Laminate it to ensure durability. Players will also need several tokens and scratch paper. In the center of the game board there are six numbers. Players may choose to add any combination of these numbers. This game is to be played by two players. To begin the game each player selects one of the paths leading away from the center. Player A then adds any combination of the numbers in the center. If the sum results in one of the totals on his/her path, he/she may place a token on that number. If the total is found on the path of the opponent, the opponent gets to place a token on the number. There are obviously some combinations not found on either path. Players alternate taking turns and making choices of addends. The first player to cover all of the numbers on his/her path with tokens wins.

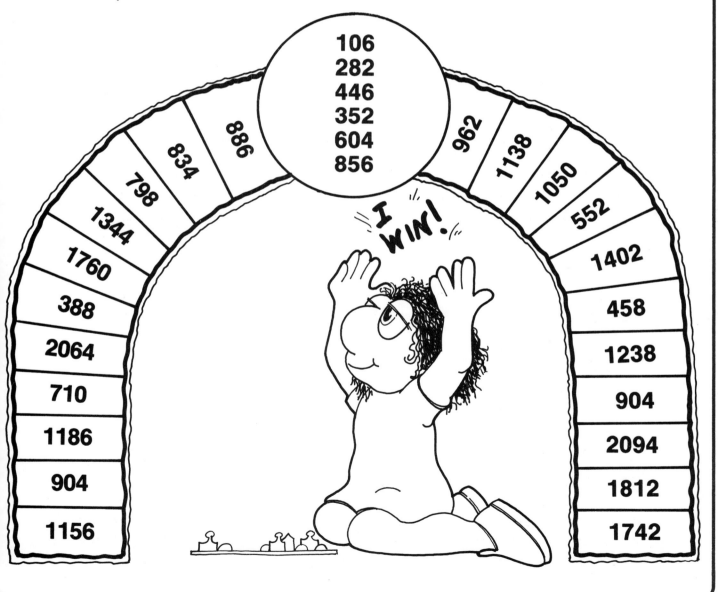

39

GA279

BALANCING BOXES

Balance the boxes below so that they all contain three numbers. . .the sum of which is the same for each box. Two of the boxes already contain two numbers, so they will need only one number each. The other three boxes contain only one number each, so each of these boxes will need two numbers.

Choose from the list of numbers below. You may use each number only one time. . .and you will have just enough numbers to complete all the boxes and make them equal.

2, 5, 10, 14, 15, 16, 17, 21

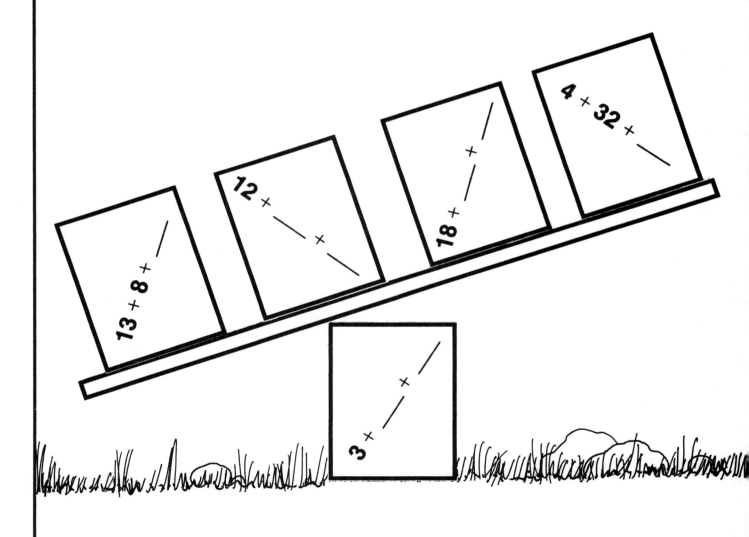

GA27

INDEPENDENT STUDY CARDS (ANIMALS)

Groups of Animals
A large number of kangaroos gathered together

617	63	496	1089	346
363	812	340	95	690
547	78	79	341	999
O	P	T	U	R

| 915 | 2035 | 1527 | 1525 | 953 |

Groups of Animals
A gathering of geese

319	19	436	688	982	436
444	999	519	488	46	886
819	319	83	87	506	402
G	L	G	E	G	A

| 1038 | 1724 | 1534 | 1582 | 1337 | 1263 |

Groups of Animals
Turkeys grouped together

66	813	552	742	111	88
88	409	6	918	223	919
119	737	78	1078	599	202
39	412	348	309	17	727
E	F	A	R	R	T

| 950 | 984 | 2371 | 1936 | 312 | 3047 |

Groups of Animals
Many, many wise owls all gathered together

413	36	182	139	809
583	42	46	239	1012
919	912	312	593	780
836	3	299	618	309
707	967	119	101	1007
L	P	M	T	N

436	605	866	166	380
398	300	1205	342	200
599	19	309	981	0
605	509	309	134	400
119	286	433	314	909
A	A	I	R	E

| 1960 | 1719 | 1937 | 3458 | 3417 | 2157 | 958 | 1889 | 3917 | 1690 |

41

GA279

_____ is hereby
awarded the
CHECKERED FLAG

for finishing ahead of time in math.

_____
(teacher)

_____ WINS

THE BUSY BEAVER AWARD **for work in math.**

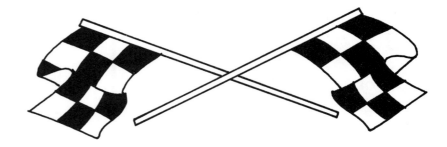

_____
(teacher)

42

GA2

DESTRUCTO DIVISION

Make the background of this bulletin board out of a light colored construction paper or poster board. The idea is for the teacher to show children the mechanics involved in the process of division. The large rocks serve as the dividends, so be certain that they can be evenly divided. Choose one of the factors to serve as the "crusher" on the machine. The other factor shows the number of smaller rocks (the quotient) that results when the actual division takes place. Another possible use of this bulletin board would be for the teacher to develop the "crusher" and choose the large rock (dividend); then let the students tell how many smaller rocks would result.

LINCOLN TIMES

Make the background for this bulletin board out of a light colored construction paper or tag board. You can use any newspaper for the newspaper in the foreground, but it creates a greater impact on the students if you use a copy of the school newspaper. The title should also reflect your particular school.

The letters for the title can either be made from colored construction paper or old newspapers pasted down and outlined with a black felt-tipped marker.

Place flash cards at random over the rest of the board. This board makes an excellent addition to your multiplication/division learning center, since it is mainly an attention-catching board.

44

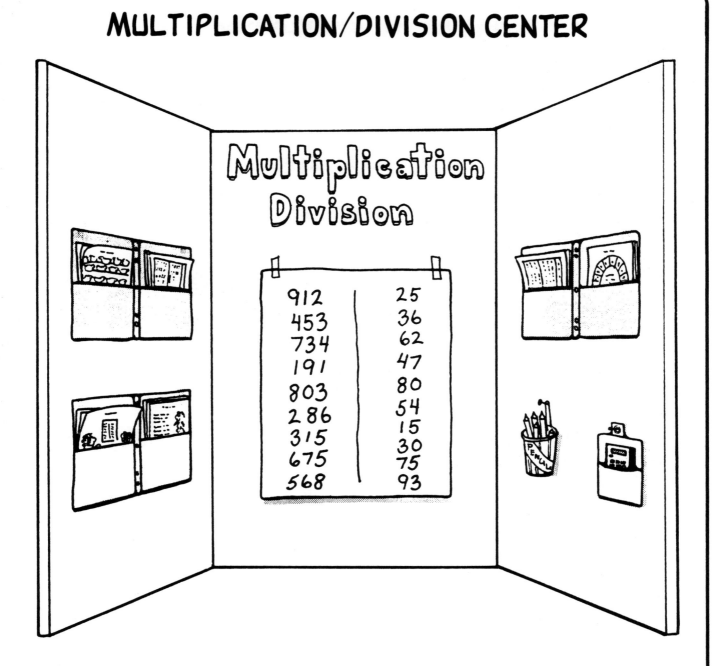

After covering game boards with Con-Tact paper to ensure durability, it's also a good idea to place all gameboards and pieces into separate folders. Use regular file folders and staple at both ends to keep each game or idea intact. Attach instructions for playing the game or completing the activity securely on the inside of the folder or on the back. Stickers or pictures or decorative lettering also help to enhance the appeal of the learning center.

It is also appropriate to maintain a chart for use in cross checking those tasks which have been completed by each child in each learning center.

45

TIMES TO REMEMBER

This exercise is a good one for practicing one-digit division problems. Using 3" x 5" index cards, put one of the following numbers on each card with a black felt-tipped marking pen:

8, 16, 24, 32, 40, 48, 56, 64, 72,
9, 18, 27, 36, 45, 54, 63, 72, 81

63

I wonder. . . is the divisor 9?

Shuffle the cards for a drill in division by 8 and 9. Players alternate choosing cards. When a player chooses a card, he/she then tries to think of both the dividend and the quotient that will answer the dividend. For example, if a 63 is drawn, the student then must reflect on whether the divisor is 8 or 9. This creates a "flash" review of the 8 and 9 multiplication tables. Hopefully, the students will associate 63 with the 9's and come up with a quotient of 7. The other player obviously serves as checker (getting the same type of practice). It's better to play this game as a drill exercise than as a game with an actual winner.

The drill can be used for any of the multiplication tables singly, in groups of two, or perhaps, near the end of the year, the dividends could include several of the multiplication tables.

GA279

DOUBLE YOUR PLEASURE

You've often heard the wise old statement about how . . . "a penny saved is a penny earned." But, since a penny doesn't really buy very much these days, perhaps you didn't pay much attention to it. If so, then try this statement: "A penny doubled each day makes a man *very, very* rich!" In fact, you might be really amazed at just how much money you could accumulate in just one month (30 days) if you doubled your money every day. Let's just see how much.

As you look at the examples in the chart below, you aren't going to believe this is true. So you'll just have to finish the chart to really find out.

You can use scratch paper to figure your answers when they get into really big numbers. Then put down all your findings in the chart below. Along about the 20th or 21st day you'll begin to see how really big this is going to get.

Day	Amount of $	Day	Amount of $
1	.01	16	
2	.02	17	
3	.04	18	
4	.08	19	
5	.16	20	
6		21	
7		22	
8		23	
9		24	
10		25	
11		26	
12		27	
13		28	
14		29	
15		30	

Makes you want to start saving your pennies, doesn't it?

GA279

MAGIC SQUARES

Work these magic squares so that when you multiply two of the numbers either down or across, you get the third as a product.

1

2	8	
16		32

2

	5	
1		15
5		

3

6		18
	1	
3		

4

	2	
3	1	
		54

5

3	3	
	6	6

GA279

RUNNING REMAINDERS

Construct a game board similar to the one below. To play this game, players need one pair of dice, a token for each player and scratch paper for each player. Players roll dice to determine the order of play. The high roller begins the game by rolling the dice, then adding the two together. This number becomes the divisor. The number on the board where the player is located serves as the *dividend*. The player then performs the division on scratch paper and moves the number of spaces indicated in the remainder of the quotient.

If, for example, the first player rolls a 6 and a 5 (for a total of 11), the problem is one of dividing 146 by 11. This yields a quotient of 13 with a remainder of 3. The player would then move his/her token three spaces and play advances to the next player. The next time it is his/her turn, he/she will roll again and divide 173 by whatever divisor is indicated by the dice. If a player works a problem which doesn't yield any remainder, then his/her token does not move until the next turn. The first player to reach the finish line is the winner.

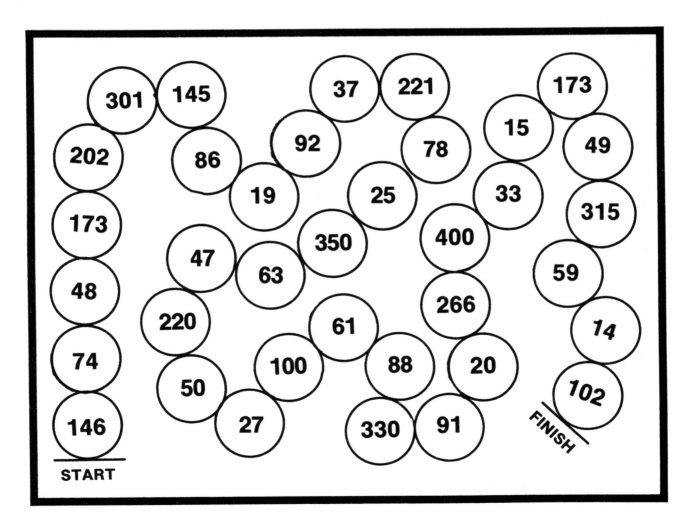

49

MARATHON

Construct a game board similar to the board shown below and on the next page. Laminate it to ensure the game's durability.

Each player will need a sheet of scratch paper and several tokens.

Each player is playing against time, so play is on an individual basis. Simply note the time when a student starts and when he/she finishes.

To begin the game, a player chooses a number from the pool of dividends and a number from the pool of divisors. The player then completes the division on scratch paper. After finding the answer, the player then finds the quotient on the track and covers that number with a token.

FINISH LINE

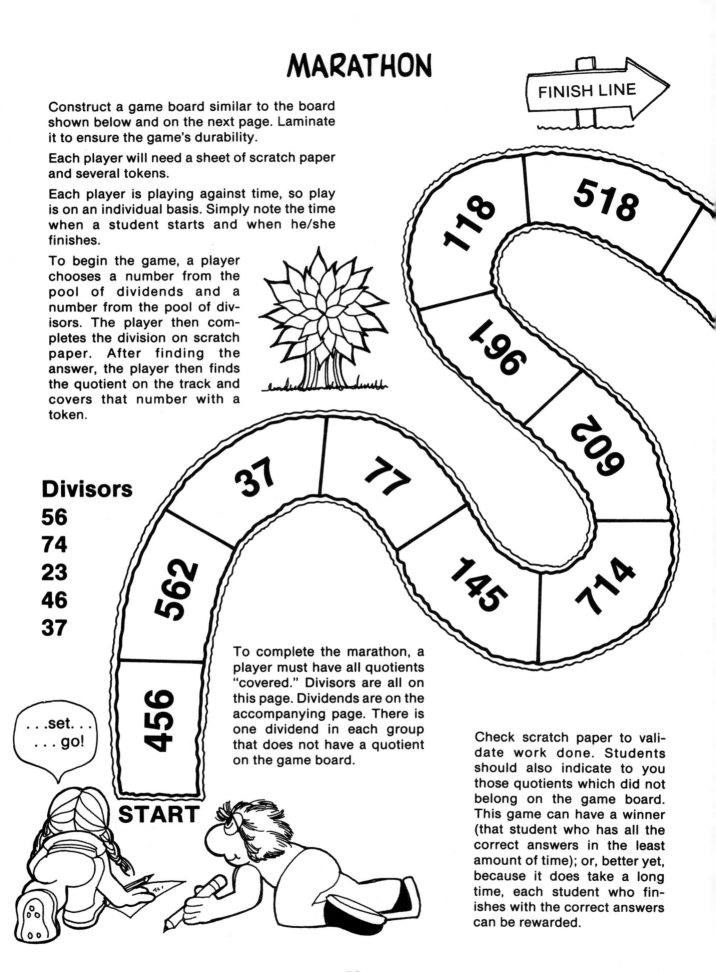

518

118

196

209

37

77

145

714

562

456

Divisors
56
74
23
46
37

...set...
...go!

START

To complete the marathon, a player must have all quotients "covered." Divisors are all on this page. Dividends are on the accompanying page. There is one dividend in each group that does not have a quotient on the game board.

Check scratch paper to validate work done. Students should also indicate to you those quotients which did not belong on the game board. This game can have a winner (that student who has all the correct answers in the least amount of time); or, better yet, because it does take a long time, each student who finishes with the correct answers can be rewarded.

GA279

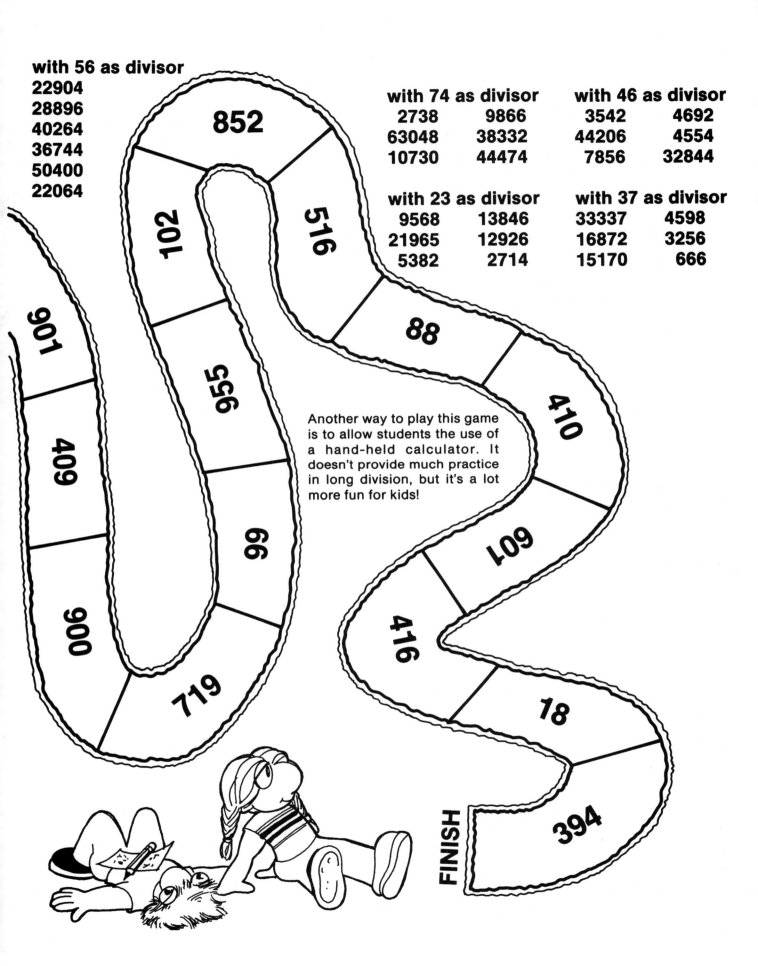

with 56 as divisor
22904
28896
40264
36744
50400
22064

with 74 as divisor
2738   9866
63048   38332
10730   44474

with 46 as divisor
3542   4692
44206   4554
7856   32844

with 23 as divisor
9568   13846
21965   12926
5382   2714

with 37 as divisor
33337   4598
16872   3256
15170   666

852
102
516
955
88
410
66
609
719
416
18
394
901
409
900

Another way to play this game is to allow students the use of a hand-held calculator. It doesn't provide much practice in long division, but it's a lot more fun for kids!

FINISH

51

MILEAGE MATH

Compute the cost of a tank full of gas. The tank holds 22 gallons and the gasoline costs $1.14/gallon for the unleaded fuel it requires. If the tank is completely empty, how much would it cost to fill it up?

If this car can travel 561 miles on that tank of gas, how many miles per gallon is the car getting? This *miles per gallon* figure is really important to car owners.

Once you've finished figuring the *miles per gallon*, compute the cost of the gasoline per mile. Do this by dividing the total cost of the gas by the number of miles traveled.

Car owners are very much concerned about how far their cars will go on a tank of gas these days. That just makes sense, because the farther they can go per tank, the less it's going to cost them to get there.

GA279

What are some things people who own cars can do to make their trips cost less?

_____

_____

_____

_____

What effect do you suppose driving 55 miles per hour has on the *miles per gallon* when compared to a car that is going 65 miles per hour?

Do you suppose the slower car gets *better mileage*?

Millions of Americans buy smaller cars simply because they get better gas mileage. What advantage does a bigger car have over a smaller car?

Why have states decided to allow people to drive 65 miles per hour on interstate highways?

If we buy one of these sub-compact cars that gets *38 miles per gallon*, how much money is saved on the 561 mile trip with the smaller car (see problem on p. 52)?

Now that you have considered all the angles, what type of car would you buy right now if you were old enough to buy one and you had the money?

GA279

SHADY OAKS COUNTRY CLUB

This game can be played by two, three or four players.

To play the game you need a scorecard and a pair of dice.

HOLE	PAR	FRONT 9			HOLE	PAR	BACK 9		
1	4				10	4			
2	3				11	4			
3	3				12	4			
4	4				13	3			
5	4				14	4			
6	5				15	4			
7	4				16	4			
8	4				17	3			
9	4				18	5			
TOTAL					TOTAL				

Each "hole" presents a math problem that can be solved by rolling the dice. The number of rolls necessary to complete the problem is the score for that hole.

54

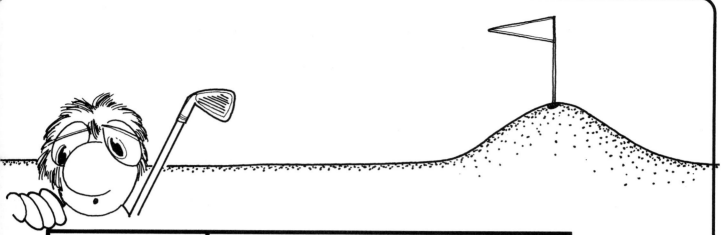

1st hole	Roll an "ace" on either cube
2nd hole	Roll a combination whose sum is greater than 10
3rd hole	Roll a combination that totals exactly 7
4th hole	Roll a combination that. . .when multiplied. . .yields a product of 24
5th hole	Roll a combination whose sum is divisible by two
6th hole	Roll a combination whose sum is exactly 5
7th hole	Roll a combination which has one die that can be divided evenly by the other die
8th hole	Roll a combination which will result in a fraction that can be further reduced
9th hole	Roll a combination whose sum is exactly 4

GA279

10th hole	**Roll a combination whose sum total is evenly divisible by 4**
11th hole	**Roll a combination that. . .when one number is subtracted from the other. . . the result is a difference of 2**
12th hole	**Roll a combination which. . .when multiplied. . .can be divided evenly by 5**
13th hole	**Roll a double number (both the same)**
14th hole	**Role a combination in which neither number can be divided evenly by 2**
15th hole	**Roll a combination. . .which. . .when multiplied together. . .results in a product that is greater than 24**
16th hole	**Roll a combination which. . .when multiplied. . .results in a product that is less than 6**
17th hole	**Roll a combination whose sum is exactly 10**
18th hole	**Roll a combination whose product is evenly divisible by 3**

Players roll a single die to determine the order of play (high roll is first on the "tee"). The first player then rolls the dice until he completes the requirements of the first hole. He then records the number of rolls it took him to complete that first hole. Play then passes on to the second player. When all players have completed the first hole, they proceed on to the second hole, etc. At the end of each hole, that player with the lowest score on the previous hole plays first, as he has the teeing "honor."

A round (game) can consist of either nine or eighteen holes. At the end of the agreed upon round, players total their scores. The player with the lowest score wins.

GA27

GUESSTIMATION

912	25
453	36
734	62
191	47
803	80
286	54
315	15
675	30
568	75
	93

To play this game you need a calculator (from the learning center) plus some scratch paper for each player. Give students a list of two and three digit numbers plus another list containing one and two digit numbers. As students play the game, they use a number from the *larger number list* to serve as the dividend and a number from the *smaller number list* becomes the divisor.

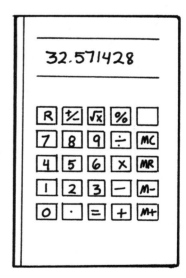

32.571428

Each player then takes a quick look at both divisor and dividend and estimates the approximate quotient. Both players write down their answers on the scratch paper. The whole idea is to come *closer* to the answer.

For example, if Player A "guesstimated" that 912 divided by 36 was about 28, he/she would divide the dividend (912) by the estimated answer (28) and get 32.571428 as an answer. He/She then subtracts the divisor (36) from this figure and gets a score of -3.428572. Let's say Player B thought that 912 divided by 36 would come closer to 24. He/She then divides the 912 by the chosen "guesstimate" of 24 and gets a result of 38. He/She then subtracts the divisor (36) from that number and gets 2.000. Player B's answer is closer to the real answer of 25 than Player A's answer. .. thus Player B wins that round.

GA279

CLEARING LOW HURDLES

Construct the game board of tagboard and laminate it or cover it with Con-Tact paper. Make spaces large enough to enable students to write in answers to problems easily. Provide grease pencils so that answers can be wiped clean and problems changed.

tagboard

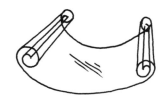

clear Con-Tact paper

grease pencils

Two players can play this game and each should be given a token before beginning. Prepare the game board by writing problems on each hurdle similar to those below. At the start of the game each player begins by marking down his/her answers on the spaces marked after each hurdle.

The first player to the finish line wins the race. If he/she should "trip" over any hurdles along the way (misses a problem), then the other hurdler wins the race. Students can check the work of each other as additional practice.

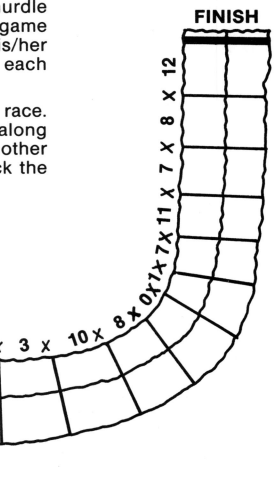

RUNNER A
MULTIPLY 6

RUNNER B
MULTIPLY 7

START

GA27

This same idea can be adapted for use by older children by simply making the problems more difficult. For example, 6 × 232, 6 × 541, etc. If you use the game this way, students should be given scratch paper for calculating their answers.

Play can also be on an individual basis with the hurdler trying to better previous time for completing the race. This provides an excellent drill activity for students who are learning the multiplication tables.

GA279

CLASSIFIED MATH

WANT ADS

HELP!

Earn extra spending $$$ after school stuffing envelopes. Fast workers will really "lick" this job. Piece work. 2 cents/envelope.

How much can Tom and Bill earn in four hours if they average six envelopes per minute each?

FOR SALE

Slightly used 10-speed bicycle. Owner needs $$$ fast! $50 off original price of $170. Only five months old. Priced to sell now! Great deal!

How much for the bicycle? How much per month did it cost the owner to have the bicycle if he/she can sell it for what he/she wants?

SAVE $$$$

Buy student season pass for only $6.75. See all 9 home games. Regular admission. . .$1.50 per game. Save $$$$

How much do you save over the whole season? What is the cost per game?

FOR RENT

School gym available for rent on weekends and evenings. Put your group "on the run" for only $10/hour.

How much will it cost for three evenings per week for 2 hours each evening?

CHEERLEADER CAR WASH

Help students go to cheerleading camp!

Duffy's Station, Saturday from 8-4. $2.50/car. . . $3.00/truck. . . $5.00/bus

How much money if the students wash 65 cars and 116 trucks?

FOR LEASE

6th grade student willing to share old papers, tests, etc., with 5th grader. COMPLETE YEAR! Sit back and relax for only $2.50/week.

How much for this 36-week "education"?

GA27#

DEAD DUCKS

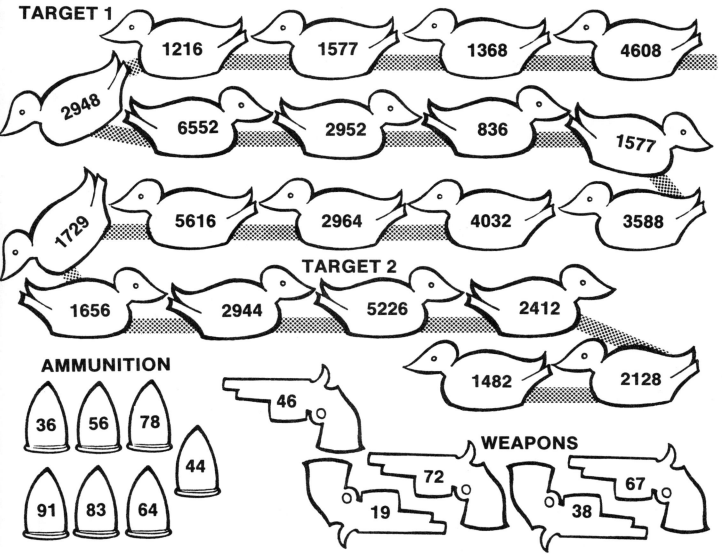

TARGET 1

1216 1577 1368 4608

2948 6552 2952 836 1577

1729 5616 2964 4032 3588

TARGET 2

1656 2944 5226 2412

1482 2128

AMMUNITION

36 56 78

44

91 83 64

46

WEAPONS

72

19 38 67

Reproduce this page for use in your multiplication-division learning center. This game is played between two players. Each will need a sheet of scratch paper and a pencil or a calculator.

The object of the game is for Player A to attempt to shoot all of Player B's ducks (Target 2) before Player B shoots all of his/her ducks (Target 1).

To begin, Player A chooses one of the weapons plus a round of ammunition and then multiplies the two together. He/She does this privately either on a sheet of scratch paper (or on a calculator if you prefer). If the product is one of B's ducks, Player A places an X on that "dead duck." If the answer is one of his/her own ducks, Player A remains quiet. He/She certainly does *not* want to shoot down his/her own ducks. After all, in a shooting gallery, the object is to shoot down the *opponent's* ducks!

MAIN STREET MATH

ANATOMY OF THE ELECTRICITY BILL

Michael's parents received these electricity bills over the past year. Their main interest seemed to be the concern of just about everybody. How much does it all cost in dollars and cents? They thought that perhaps by looking at the "whole picture," they could get some ideas about where they could save some money. They asked Michael to help them look too.

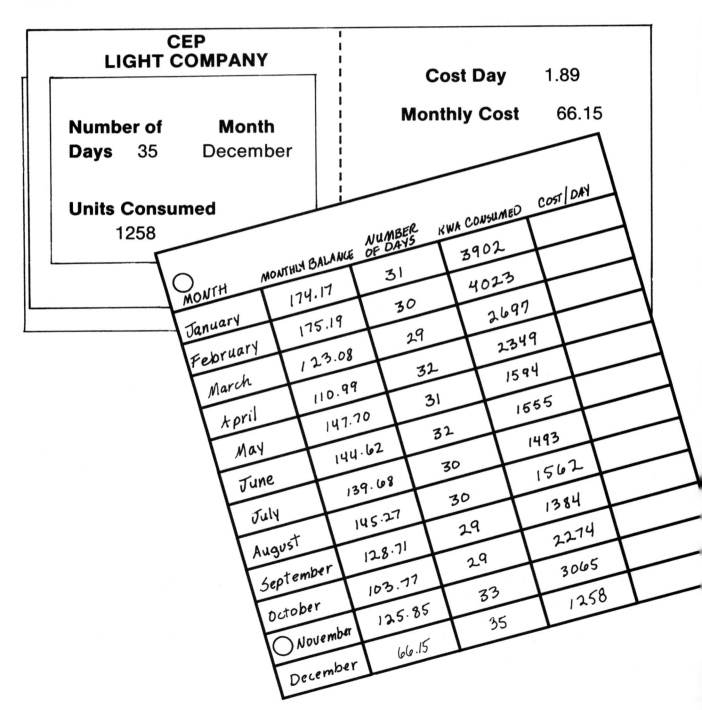

CEP LIGHT COMPANY

Number of Days	35	Month	December

Cost Day 1.89

Monthly Cost 66.15

Units Consumed 1258

MONTH	MONTHLY BALANCE	NUMBER OF DAYS	KWA CONSUMED	COST/DAY
January	174.17	31	3902	
February	175.19	30	4023	
March	123.08	29	2697	
April	110.99	32	2349	
May	147.70	31	1594	
June	144.62	32	1555	
July	139.68	30	1493	
August	145.27	30	1562	
September	128.71	29	1384	
October	103.77	29	2274	
November	125.85	33	3065	
December	66.15	35	1258	

GA279

1. Look at the bills. What was the total cost of electricity for the year?

   _____

2. How many units were consumed over the course of the entire year?

   _____

3. How many days are covered by the bills in the list? _____

4. Why do you suppose the total number of days is not in accord with a regular calendar year?

   _____

   _____

5. How much is the cost of electricity *per month*? _____

6. What was the *per day* cost of electricity for the entire year? _____

7. In which month were the most units of electricity consumed?

   _____

8. In which month was the total bill the highest? _____

9. What could explain the fact that more than twice the KWH were used in February than were used in August, yet the monthly bill for February is only about $30 higher than the August bill? (Ask around before answering this one.)

   _____

10. Looking at all this information, what kind of conclusion can you reach?

    _____

11. Are there any ways in which Michael and his parents might be able to cut the cost of their electricity bill?_____

    _____

    _____

STEAMBOAT PIZZA PORT

Holly's parents gave her the choice of having any kind of birthday party she wants. Since her very favorite food is pizza, Holly has decided to invite her friends to a pizza party at the Steamboat Pizza Port.

Her list included eleven of her best friends. Holly's mother called all of the parents and found that all of the girls could come except Cindy, who was going to be out of town that night. Both of Holly's parents will be there plus her older sister (to take pictures). So, how many people are coming altogether? Why is it important to know how many are coming?

Holly's mom called the Steamboat Pizza Port to make the necessary reservations and to ask for a sample menu. The manager said they would be given an extra special "Birthday Room'" free of charge. There would also be included without charge "Red Carpet Service" complete with party favors, free juke box music and sirens. Finally, there would even be a birthday cake complete with candles.

There would, however, be a charge of $1.50 per serving for the "Double Header" (a two-dip sundae with a special topping). The manager also wanted to know the time of arrival, the number coming and the pizzas that would be ordered. The reason was that the Steamboat would go ahead and start the pizzas ahead of time. They would then be ready shortly after the group's arrival.

STEAMBOAT PIZZA PORT!
MAY I TAKE YOUR ORDER, PLEASE?

GA279

Holly's mom received this menu in the next day's mail.

Steamboat Pizza Port

	small	medium	large
CHEESE	$4.00	$5.00	$6.50
GREEN PEPPER	4.50	5.50	7.25
SAUERKRAUT	4.50	5.50	7.25
ONION	4.50	5.50	7.25
ANCHOVY	4.50	5.50	7.25
PEPPERONI	4.50	5.50	7.25
MUSHROOM	4.50	5.50	7.25
HAMBURGER	4.50	5.50	7.25
SAUSAGE	4.50	5.50	7.25
HAM	4.50	5.50	7.25
CANADIAN BACON	4.50	5.50	7.25
GREEN OLIVE	4.50	5.50	7.25
TACO	5.25	6.50	7.75
TWO-ITEM PIZZA	5.00	6.25	8.25
STEAMBOAT SPECIAL	6.00	7.50	8.50
EXTRA ITEM	.50	.75	1.00
DOUBLE CHEESE	.75	1.00	1.25
STEAMBOAT DELUXE	7.00	8.00	9.00

Soft drinks are sold in quantities of $.90 each or by the pitcher for $2.75.

After looking it over, she and Holly decided how many pizzas to order. After some tough decision making on which kinds of pizza to order and how much, Holly's mom phoned in the following order:

1 large sausage and mushroom
1 large Canadian bacon
1 medium taco
1 medium (½ pepperoni and ½ ham)

They also ordered three pitchers of soda pop.

GA279

When the party was over, Holly's dad left the girl who served them a $10.00 tip for cleaning up their mess. Everyone also had a "Double Header." The sales tax amounts to 6% except for the tip. What was the total cost of Holly's birthday party?

Do your figuring here.

After you've finished working out the costs of Holly's party, make up a party of your own using the same menu. After deciding how many will be in your party, decide what should be ordered and figure out the total cost. Be sure not to "under-order." You don't want friends leaving hungry. On the other hand, food is expensive today, and you don't want your party to cost your parents more than is necessary. Calculate the total cost including tax and tip. Then you can exchange your plans with other members of your class. Don't figures like this make you appreciate why your parents can't afford to have a lot of parties?

GA279

Find the answers for each of the following problems. After calculating the answers, begin at START position with a pencil and complete the drawing.

3 × 6
4 × 5
7 × 3
8 × 4
9 × 1
6 × 2
2 × 5
5 × 5
8 × 3
7 × 1
8 × 2
5 × 2
6 × 1
4 × 3
3 × 3

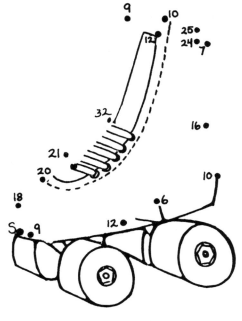

Find the answers for each of the following problems. After calculating the answers, begin at START position with a pencil and complete the drawing.

5 × 4
3 × 1
3 × 8
9 × 4
7 × 6
8 × 4
5 × 3
4 × 9
7 × 5
4 × 2
8 × 9
9 × 1
4 × 6
5 × 8
2 × 9

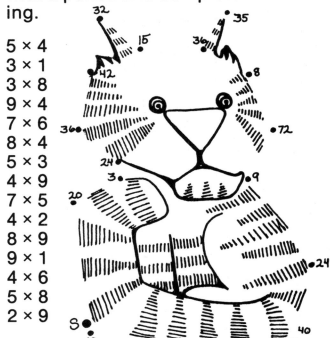

Find the answers for each of the following problems. After calculating the answers, begin at START position with a pencil and complete the drawing.

7 × 4
3 × 7
9 × 5
5 × 7
4 × 8
7 × 8
4 × 2
2 × 8
3 × 9
9 × 8
6 × 5
6 × 3
7 × 2
8 × 1
9 × 9

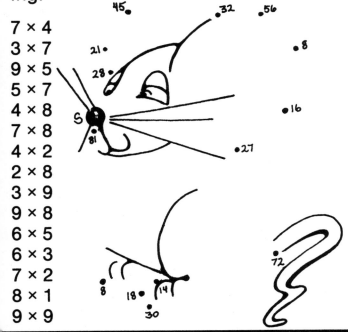

Find the answers for each of the following problems. After calculating the answers, begin at START position with a pencil and complete the drawing.

2 × 5
4 × 7
7 × 7
8 × 3
4 × 4
3 × 3
7 × 8
4 × 5
6 × 9
7 × 5
2 × 8
6 × 8
4 × 6
3 × 5
2 × 7

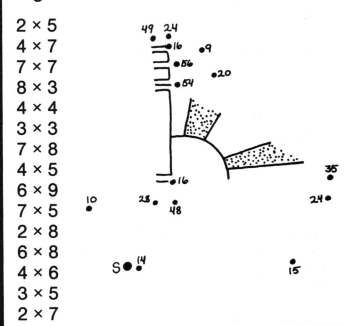

He won the 1980 New York City Marathon in record time in his first marathon ever.

341 | 262 | 453 | 777 | 124 | 985 | 422 | | 123 | 188 | 177 | 455 | 356 | 95 | 210

FIRST NAME

L 42)11004 R 16)1984 B 26)11778 A 68)23188 E 12)9324

O 68)28696 T 49)48265

SURNAME

Z 14)4984 A 36)6768 L 25)4425 A 98)9310

A 82)37310 R 67)14070 S 85)10455

He has won more money playing golf than anyone else.

89 | 63 | 41 | 52 | | 13 | 78 | 11 | 33 | 52 | 22 | 61 | 14

FIRST NAME

J 418)37202 K 618)32136 C 633)25953 A 581)36603

SURNAME

K 567)18711 S 654)9156 U 825)50325 N 410)5330 I 60)4680

L 633)32916 C 111)1221 A 333)7326

She won 125 consecutive tennis matches on clay between 1973-1974—the longest streak by any player on any surface.

355 | 477 | 142 | 368 | 96 | 455 | 186 | 878 | 640 | 318

FIRST NAME

I 45)16560 C 88)31240 S 78)7488 R 63)8946 H 18)8586

SURNAME

E 99)45045 R 55)35200 T 74)23532 V 22)4092 E 21)18438

He was banned from baseball for life in 1989 for betting on his team.

18 | 29 | 72 | 32 | 95 | 14 | 71 | 62

FIRST NAME

E 810 23490 P 963 17334 E 630 20160 T 321 23112

SURNAME

S 255 18105 R 886 84170 E 174 10788 O 332 4648

68

GA279

DUGOUT DATA

number of bases in the diamond
÷ the number of innings in a game
× the number of players on one team
÷ the number of bases covered in a single
÷ the number of bases covered in a double
÷ the number of bases covered in a triple
× the number of bases covered in a home run
× the number of teams in the major leagues
× the number of bases advanced in a Grand Slam
÷ the number of games a team must win to win the World Series

BASEBALL SPORTS SHORTS

THE 19th HOLE

the number of holes in a round of golf
× the score for an "ace"
× the score for a bogey on a par 4 hole
× a score of birdie on a par 3 hole
÷ a score of eagle on a par 5 hole
× the maximum number of clubs one can carry
× the number of holes in a PGA tournament
÷ a double bogey on a par 4
÷ a double eagle on a par 5 hole
÷ the number of tournaments in the Grand Slam

GOLF SPORT SHORTS

THE END ZONE

the number of minutes in an NFL game
÷ the number of quarters in a game
× the number of points for a safety
÷ the number of points for a touchdown
× the number of points for a field goal
× the length of a football field in yards
÷ the number of yards needed for a first down
× the number of teams in the NFL

FOOTBALL SPORT SHORTS

THE FIFTH FOUL

number of halves in a game
× the number of players on one team
× the length of a college game in minutes
× the distance of the free throw line
÷ the number of referees in a college game
÷ the time limit when the ball must be brought over the center stripe
× the number of games a team must win to win a 16-team tournament
÷ the number of minutes played during overtime periods of college games

BASKETBALL SPORTS SHORTS

GA279

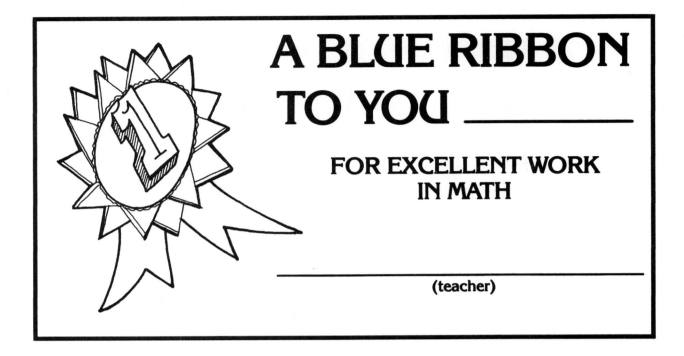

A BLUE RIBBON TO YOU _____

FOR EXCELLENT WORK IN MATH

_____
(teacher)

_____

is right on TARGET IN MATH

_____
(teacher)

FRACTION/ACTION

Place these or other similar real life fractions in action on a bulletin board to attract student interest. Ask students to decide which fractions are shown in the various situations by going over the entire board in class. Ask questions like. . .What part is gone? What fraction has been consumed? What part remains?

GA279

FRACTION/DECIMAL CENTER

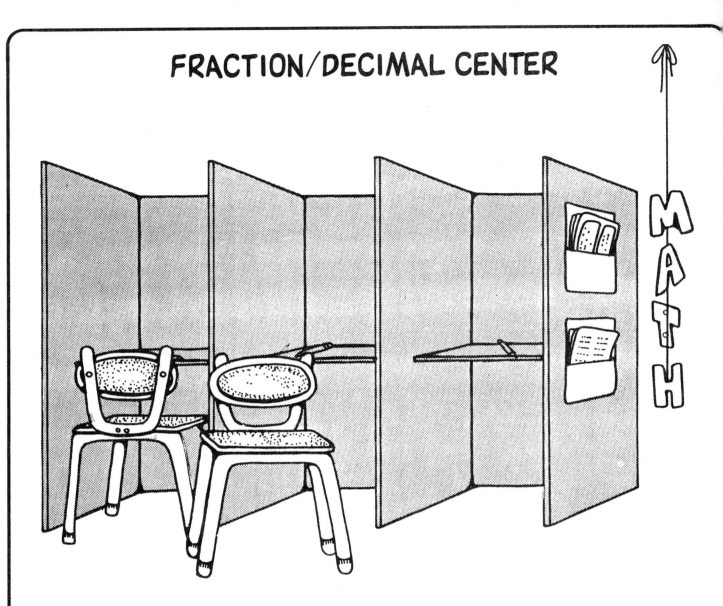

Learning centers should provide not only enrichment, but should also serve to stimulate student interest as well. It is important to note that when using centers for enrichment or skill building purposes, there must first be an adequate explanation from the teacher of the techniques involved. Without proper direction, student experiences in the learning center can end in frustration and little accomplishment. One of the more positive spin-offs of the learning center approach is that children learn how to better manage their own time more efficiently. Those students who are successful in this respect often learn better self-discipline and control over their other study habits.

Study carrels are very effective in creating a learning center and they have the added advantage of providing perhaps the very best chance for placing students in a work environment which they really feel is their own (if only for the moment). Their major drawback is their cost, but this can often be cut considerably with a handy carpenter and an abundant supply of plywood.

GA27

TRACKING FRACTIONS

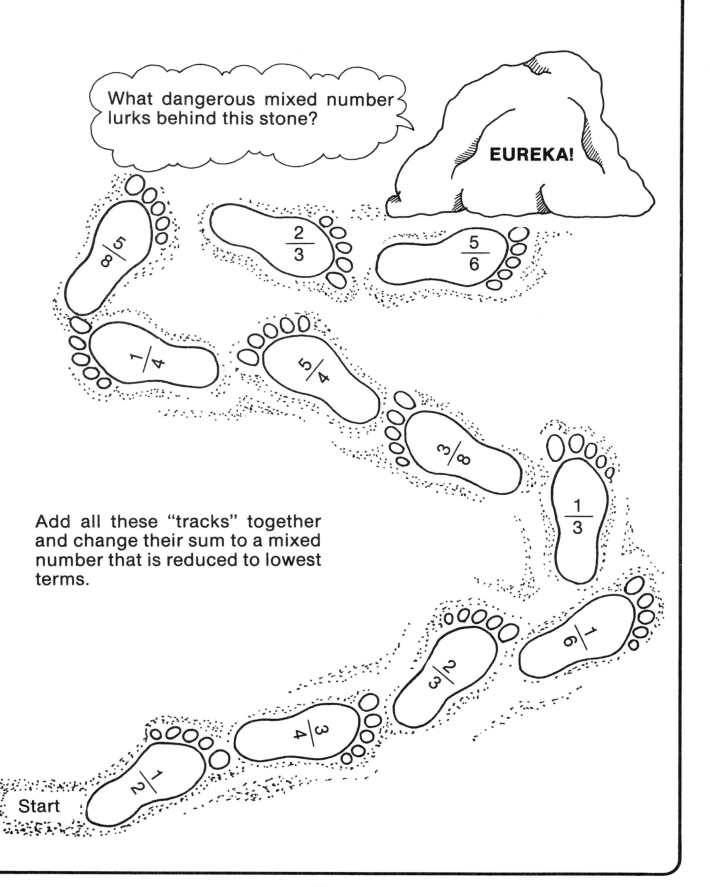

What dangerous mixed number lurks behind this stone?

EUREKA!

$\frac{5}{8}$

$\frac{2}{3}$

$\frac{5}{6}$

$\frac{1}{4}$

$\frac{5}{4}$

$\frac{3}{8}$

$\frac{1}{3}$

Add all these "tracks" together and change their sum to a mixed number that is reduced to lowest terms.

$\frac{1}{6}$

$\frac{2}{3}$

$\frac{3}{4}$

$\frac{1}{2}$

Start

GA279

COLORED FRACTIONS

Color each area below with the indicated color of marker or crayon. Then look closely at the areas you have colored. What fractional part of the squares does the area occupied by each of the colors represent?

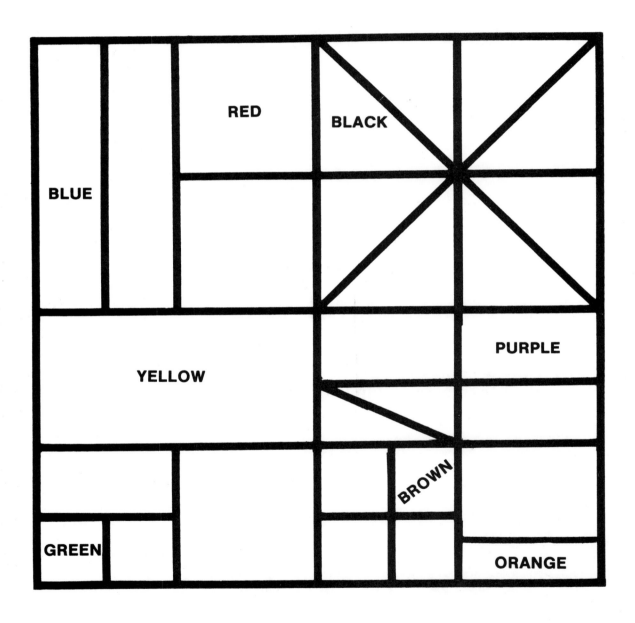

GA27

HIDDEN ANIMAL

Find the hidden animal in the puzzle below by shading in all areas that contain fractions reduced to lowest terms. Leave unshaded those areas containing fractions that can be further reduced.

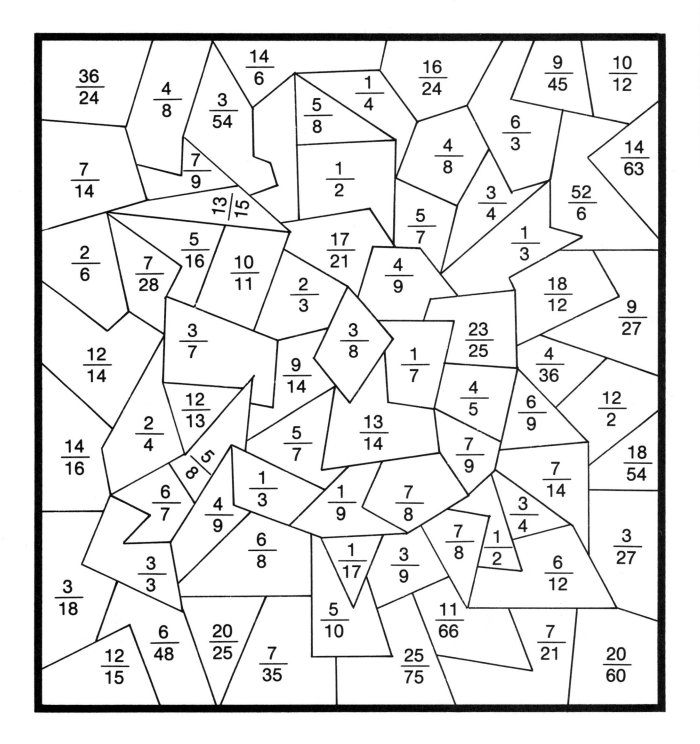

GA279

FOLDED FRACTIONS

To "fold fractions" you should begin with a number of circles that are all the same size. Use a circular pizza pan for the outline and cut out several circular shapes on plain white paper. You will also need paste and either construction paper or tagboard for pasting down your "folded fractions." Finally, you will need a black felt-tipped pen and colored markers if you want to make your fractions more attractive.

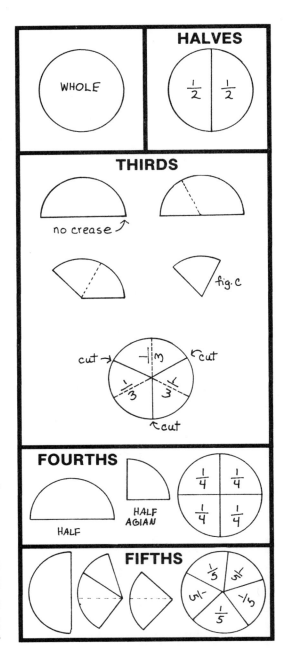

WHOLE: Leave it just like it is.

HALVES: Fold circle in half and cut along fold. Paste on paper and label each half.

THIRDS: Fold circle in half, but do not crease fold. Now fold ⅓ of the top ½ on top of the other ⅔. Then fold over other third as in figure C. You now have a circle that is divided into sixths. To make thirds, simply cut along the crease of every other fold. Paste on paper and label each third.

FOURTHS: Fold circle in half first. Then fold in half again to get circle into four equal parts. Cut apart on folds, paste on paper and label each fourth.

FIFTHS: Fold circle in half. Then fold ⅖ of top over ⅗ of top. Next fold remaining ⅕ over already folded ⅘. You now have paper folded into tenths. Cut along every other crease. Paste on paper and label each fifth.

GA2

SIXTHS: Use same procedures as for thirds except that you should cut along every fold this time. Paste on paper and label each sixth.

SEVENTHS: Fold circle in half. Then fold ³⁄₇ of top over ⁴⁄₇. Take remaining ¹⁄₇ and fold it over the already-folded ⁶⁄₇ as shown in figure. Open folds and cut along every other line. Paste on paper and label each seventh.

EIGHTHS: Fold a circle in half. Then fold that half in half again. Finally, fold over again. Cut along each crease, paste on paper and label each eighth.

NINTHS: Use same procedure as you used to get thirds (and sixths) except before you unfold thirds, fold ¹⁄₃ over a final time. Then fold the uncovered third on top of the whole and you will have the circle divided into eighteenths. Cut along every other fold, paste onto paper and label each ninth.

TENTHS: Use the same folds as you used for creating fifths except that you should fold the whole thing in half one more time. Cut along every folded crease, paste onto paper and label each tenth.

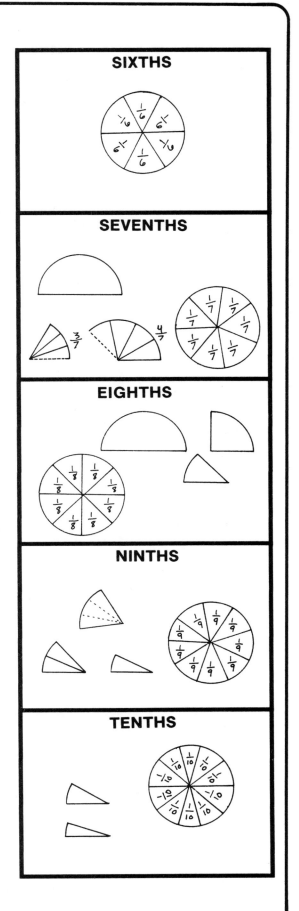

GA279

SUNDAY AFTERNOON PERCENTAGES

Below are the standings at the end of the eleventh week in the National Football League.

American Conference East			
New England	8	3	0
Buffalo	7	4	0
Indianapolis	6	5	0
Miami	6	5	0
N.Y. Jets	2	9	0
Central			
Cincinnati	8	3	0
Cleveland	7	4	0
Pittsburgh	7	4	0
Houston	3	8	0
West			
Oakland	8	3	0
Denver	7	4	0
Seattle	6	5	0
Kansas City	5	6	0
San Diego	4	7	0
National Conference East			
N.Y. Giants	10	1	0
Dallas	8	3	0
Washington	3	8	0
Phoenix	3	8	0
Philadelphia	3	8	0
Central			
Chicago	6	5	0
Minnesota	6	5	0
Green Bay	4	6	1
Tampa Bay	4	6	1
Detroit	4	7	0
West			
San Francisco	8	3	0
Los Angeles	7	4	0
New Orleans	3	8	0
Atlanta	0	11	0

GA27

Sportswriters publish the won-lost records of professional teams to give their readers a better idea of how far one team is either ahead or behind another. In fact, many fans have come to identify a team's standings in its league with its won-lost percentage.

Perhaps you could get a better lock on your favorite team if you understood what all those figures mean. Let's take the record of the New England Patriots. At this point in the season the Patriots have won eight of their eleven games. To calculate their won-lost percentage, simply divide the number of games won (8) by the number of games they *could have won* (11). Thus it becomes a case of 8 ÷ 11.

Note that the percentage is carried to three decimal places and then rounded off.

We could now make all these statements:
. . . that New England is winning at 72.7% of its games
. . . that New England's winning percentage is .727
. . . that New England is winning over 7 of each 10 games it plays.

Look at Green Bay's record of 4-6-1. To calculate percentages in tie games, figure it as a half-win and a half-loss. In this case 4 (wins) ÷ 11 games played = .364. Then 5 (wins) ÷ 11 games played = .454. Then add the two percentages together (.364 + .454 = .818) and divide by 2 (.818 ÷ 2); hence Green Bay's percentage is .409.

Your task now is to calculate the rest of the teams' won-lost percentages. Be certain to round off to three decimal places.

After you have finished with your calculations, answer the following questions.

1. How many percentage points is Buffalo behind New England?
2. How far are the Jets behind the Indianapolis Colts?
3. How many percentage points is Oakland ahead of Seattle?
4. How big a lead in percentage points do the Bears have over the Bucs?
5. How far is Cincinnati ahead of Pittsburgh?
6. How far are the Phoenix Cardinals behind the Dallas Cowboys?

GA279

7. How far are the Forty-Niners ahead of the Saints?
8. In the National Conference which two teams other than divisional leaders have the best won-lost percentage?
9. Of The Big Apple's (New York City) two professional football franchises, which has the better won-lost percentage record. . .and by how many percentage points?
10. Which team in the National Conference has the best won-lost percentage record?
11. What is the winning percentage of the *worst* team in the NFL?

There are many factors to be considered when trying to predict the winner in an NFL game. Home field advantage, injuries to key players, the condition of the weather, the urgency to win plus past performance against the opposition are all considered. Not to be forgotten is the team's current won-lost percentage. Using this as the *sole* basis for selecting winners, circle your *predicted* winners in next Sunday's NFL schedule.

Simply put down the percentages of both teams in the blank spaces. . . then circle the probable winners.

____ Indianapolis at New England ____
____ Chicago at Atlanta ____
____ Cincinnati at Cleveland ____
____ Detroit at Tampa Bay ____
____ Houston at New York Jets ____
____ Oakland at Philadelphia ____
____ Pittsburgh at Buffalo ____
____ Green Bay at Minnesota ____
____ Kansas City at Phoenix ____
____ Giants at San Francisco ____
____ Seattle at Denver ____
____ Washington at Dallas ____

Monday Night Football
____ Los Angeles at New Orleans ____

GA279

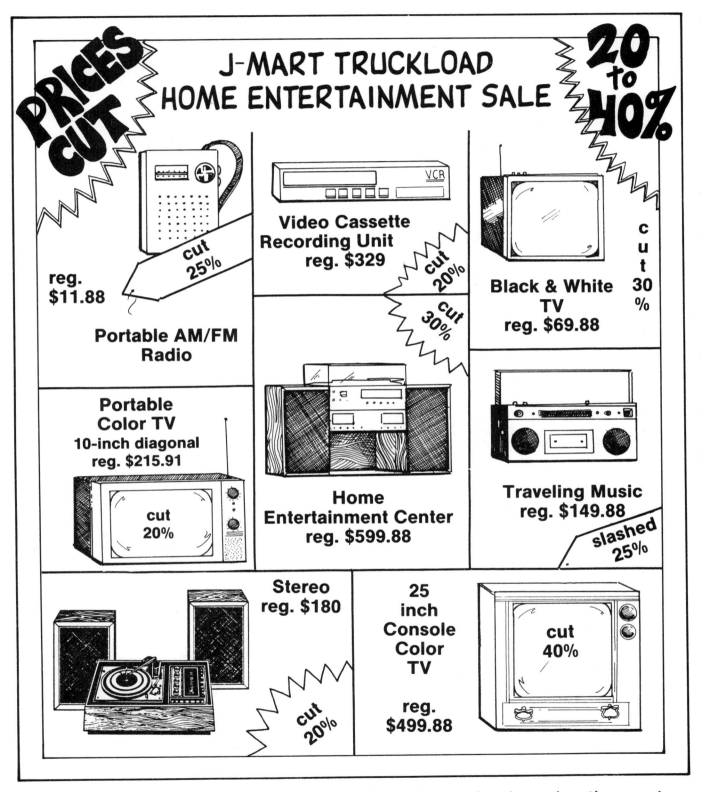

Calculate the sale price on each of the items in the advertisement. The regular price is listed plus the discounted rate. It's up to you to figure the sale price. How much is saved in each case?

GA279

WHEEL OF FRACTIONS

First, color each indicated area with correct colors (using markers, crayons or water colors). Then add together the parts that you've colored.

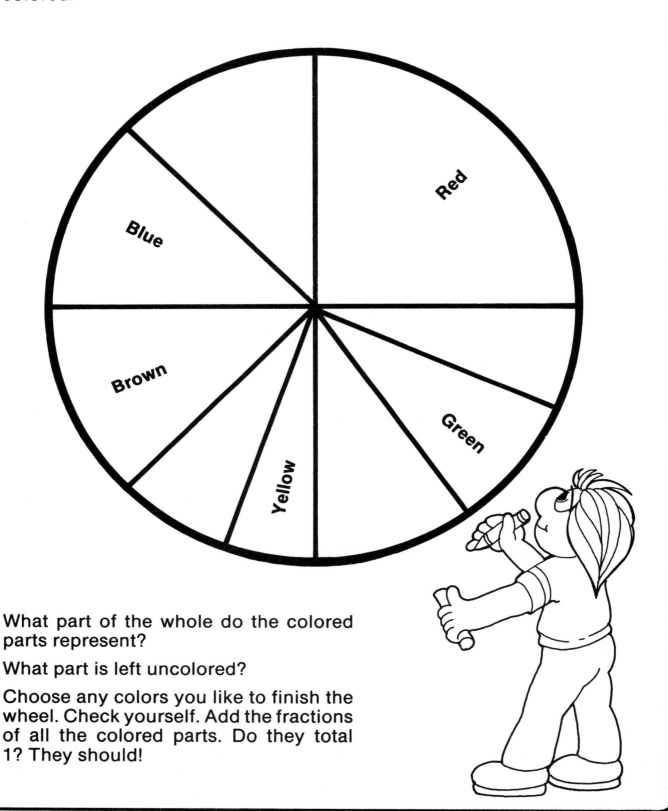

What part of the whole do the colored parts represent?

What part is left uncolored?

Choose any colors you like to finish the wheel. Check yourself. Add the fractions of all the colored parts. Do they total 1? They should!

83

The greatest selling record in history. . .selling over 100,000,000 copies since it was written in 1941.

Fraction Equivalents

16   90   45   36   24

9   64   10   30   6   12   5   36   21

1st Word: $6/9 = 9/36$ $8/11 = w/22$ $4/9 = y/81$ $9/10 = h/100$ $5/6 = j/54$

2nd Word: $1/2 = y/12$ $1/5 = m/25$ $2/5 = y/30$ $3/15 = 9/45$ $7/8 = 9/24$

$5/8 = y/48$ $8/9 = h/72$ $2/7 = y/63$ $4/7 = y/35$

He has won more gold records (for selling one million copies) than anyone else. . .116.

Decimal Equivalents

.5   .25   .6   .125   .20

.10   .333   .75   .40   .80   .1667   .67

1st Word: $1/4 = $ L $1/8 = $ I $3/5 = $ V $1/5 = $ S $1/2 = $ E

Last Word: $2/3 = $ Y $1/10 = $ P $4/5 = $ L $3/4 = $ E $1/3 = $ R $1/6 = $ E $2/5 = $ S

The all-time best seller among long-playing albums.

Fraction Equivalents

36   15   3   9   55

36   5   6   8   12   24   28

1st Word: $3/10 = 9/50$ $3/7 = N/21$ $4/9 = 9/81$ $11/12 = 9/60$ $1/4 = 4/12$

2nd Word: $7/15 = y/60$ $6/25 = 9/100$

3rd Word: $3/13 = 9/26$ $3/6 = 9/24$ $6/7 = m/42$ $1/5 = 4/25$ $2/3 = y/12$

The most successful recording artist of all time with sales of over 300,650,000 records.

Decimal Equivalents

.32   .04   .44   .28

.22   1.75   .75   .65   .15   1.4

1st Word: $11/25 = $ N $1/25 = $ I $7/25 = $ G $8/25 = $ B

2nd Word: $7/5 = $ Y $11/50 = $ C $9/8 = $ O $7/4 = $ R $3/20 = $ B $13/20 = $ S

A TIP OF THE HAT TO YOU _____

for completing your contract

_____
(teacher)

TAKE A BOW

_____

for your good work in math

_____
(teacher)

GEOBOARD GEOMETRY

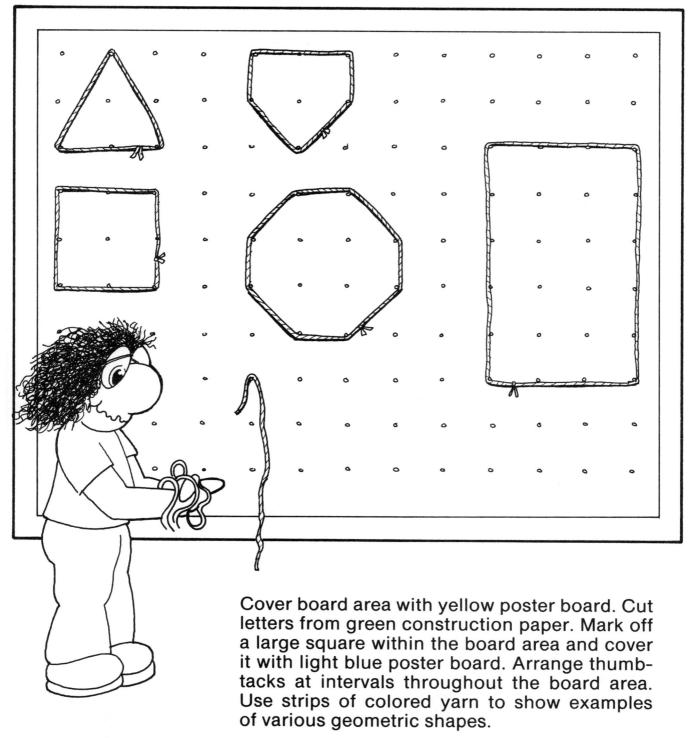

Cover board area with yellow poster board. Cut letters from green construction paper. Mark off a large square within the board area and cover it with light blue poster board. Arrange thumbtacks at intervals throughout the board area. Use strips of colored yarn to show examples of various geometric shapes.

After children have become familiar with geometric shapes and how to make them, have them design some shapes of their own using the same technique. Students can then create names for their "original" shapes.

85

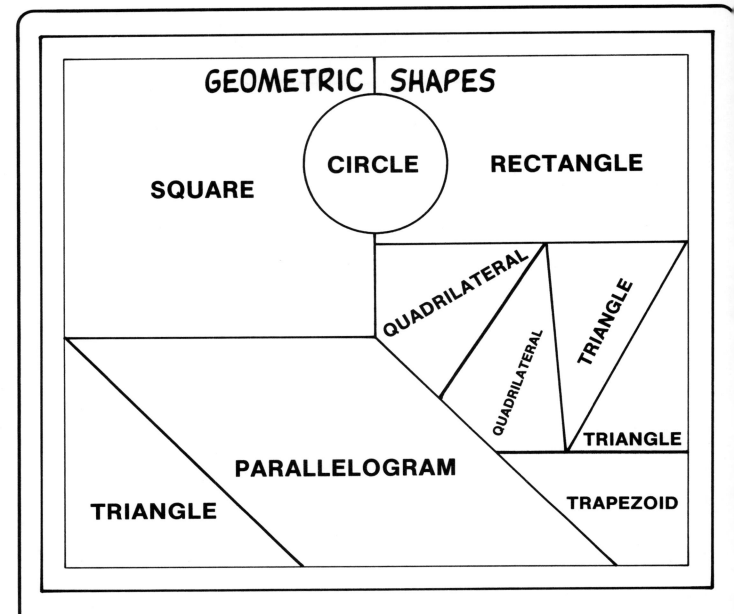

GEOMETRIC SHAPES

Another good bulletin board for attracting student interest in a study of shapes is this "wall-to-wall" collage of shapes. Using colored construction paper or colored poster board, cut out enough geometric shapes to entirely cover the board area. It doesn't matter if some overlap others since they will be of different and contrasting colors. Once you've arranged the shapes the way you want them on the board, use the flat side of a black felt-tipped marker to label each shape.

Stock your center with an ample supply of scratch paper (or construction paper or poster board if you have plenty) and let your students duplicate some of the shapes on the board. Make certain the center also has several felt-tipped markers (for labeling) and a few pairs of scissors.

86

THE LONG WAY AROUND

Measure the perimeter of each of these shapes in centimeters and place your answer on the top blank space below each figure. Then measure the same distance in inches and place that answer in the second blank below each figure. When you are finished, compare your own answers with those of other members of your class.

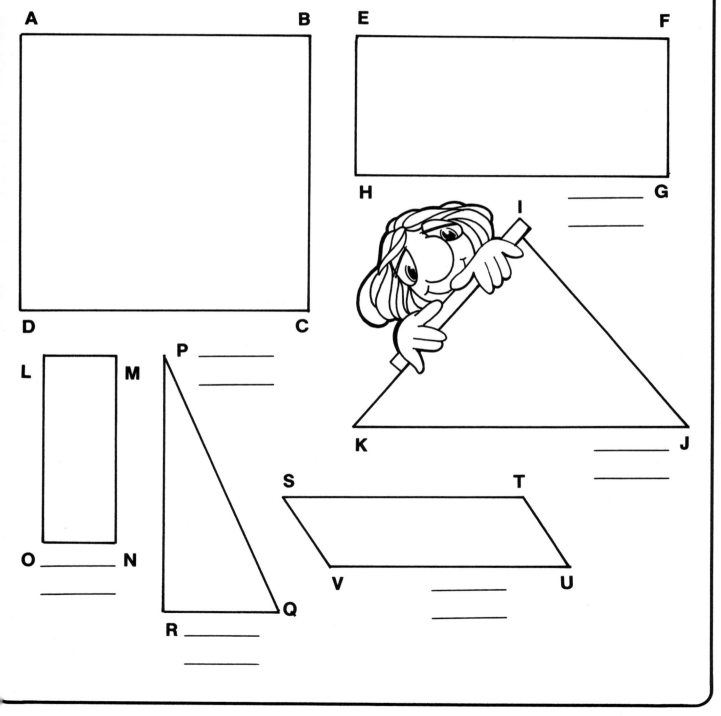

Shapes...

A *tangram* is an ancient Chinese puzzle that was made by folding a square of thin material into five triangles, a square and a rhomboid which could then be recombined to make many different figures.

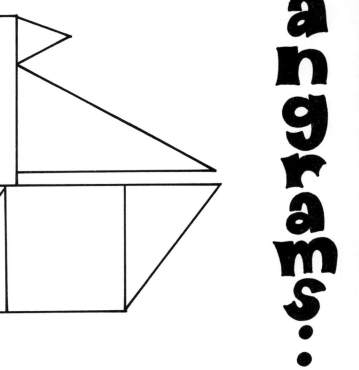

Here are seven shapes that can be cut out to make the picture above.

88

GA27

COLORED SHAPES

Color the shapes below as instructed. Then cut them out and place them on the large square below. No similar shapes (colors) or numbers may appear in the same row, the same column or the same diagonal. Put the stars on the square as shown.

Color the circles RED.
Color the squares BLUE.
Color the stars GOLD.
Color the triangles GREEN.

GA279

SIDE TO SIDE

Match the sides of the pieces of the puzzle below so that all of the problems in addition having the same answers lie adjacent to each other. When you finish, you should have a square. If not, then you've done something wrong.

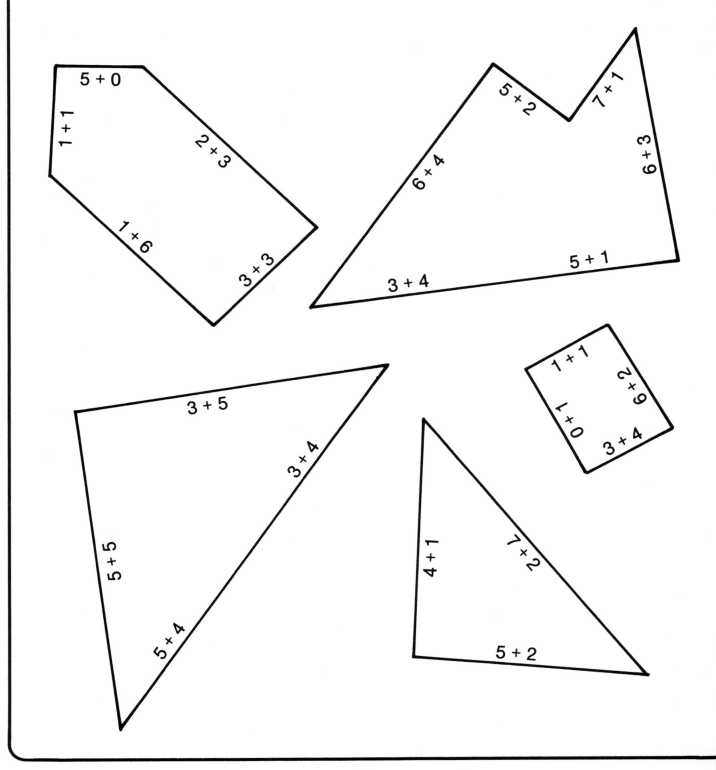

GA27

SHAPING UP

Make a very distinctive geometric shape from the following puzzle pieces by placing the sides which have the same totals next to each other. What kind of shape do you end up with?

GA279

RUBBER BAND GEOMETRY

Geoboard Geometry can be a lot of fun, but you really need to become familiar with a number of shapes before you try.

Geoboards are made of accoustical ceiling tile. Be sure you get one that will hold thumbtacks. Use large thumbtacks with big heads. You'll also need several large rubber bands.

Then do the following:

1. Show an acute angle.
2. Show an equilateral triangle.
3. Make a square.
4. Show a right angle.
5. Make two lines that are parallel to one another.
6. Make two lines that are perpendicular.
7. Make a hexagon. . .then an octagon.
8. Show a trapezoid.
9. Make a rectangle.
10. Create an obtuse angle.

Count tacks to get the perimeter of each of the above.

After you've figured the perimeter, try to calculate the area (how many "square tacks"?) of each closed figure.

Finally, create a geometric shape on your own and give it a neat name.

GA279

TAKING THE ROUND OUT OF SQUARE

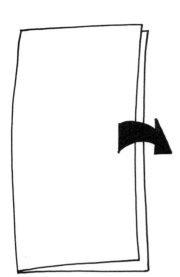

Begin by folding a square sheet of paper in half.

Then fold the paper in half again to get a folded square as shown in figure A.

Then fold diagonally to look like figure B.

Next, use a piece of string to measure off the distance between X and Y as in figure B. Keep the end of the string on X and move the other end from Y toward Z, marking the distance along the way.

Finally, cut along arc YZ and you should have a circle. Wasn't that great fun?

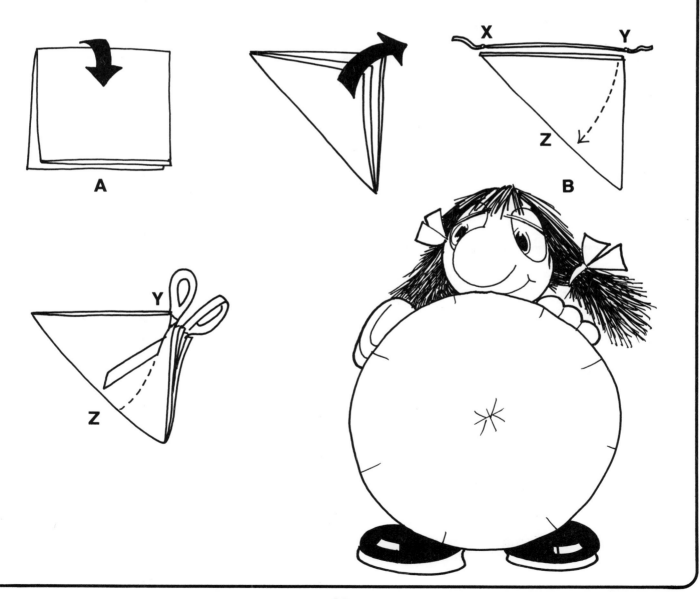

A

B

GA279

TIC-TAC SHAPE

Create enough boards similar to the board below for your entire class by cutting out several nine-inch squares from tagboard. Divide each board into nine one-inch squares with a ruler and felt-tipped pen. Then draw a single shape in each of the squares. Mix up the drawings on the boards so that you have a wide variety of different cards.

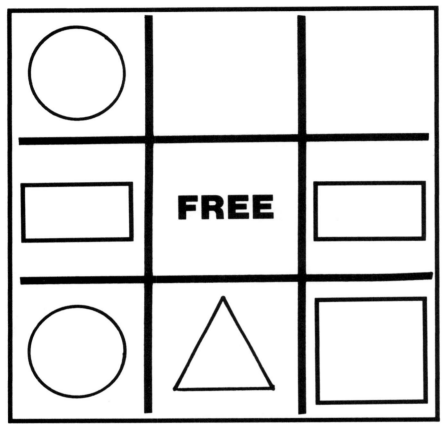

You then need to cut out several (at least 50) one-inch squares from tagboard. Draw a single shape on each one and cover with Con-Tact paper. Each player is then given several playing tokens (coins, grains of corn, etc.). The cards are shuffled and play begins with the caller drawing a single card and showing it to all players as in Bingo. Each player having that shape on his card places a token on that shape. Play continues until one player has covered three squares either vertically, horizontally or diagonally. The winner then becomes the caller for the next game.

GA27

IF THE SIDE FITS

Cut out all of the triangles below. Then fit the side of each triangle next to the side of another triangle whose side has the correct answer to the multiplication problem.

When you've finished, your triangle ought to make a square. It will if you put all the pieces in the right places.

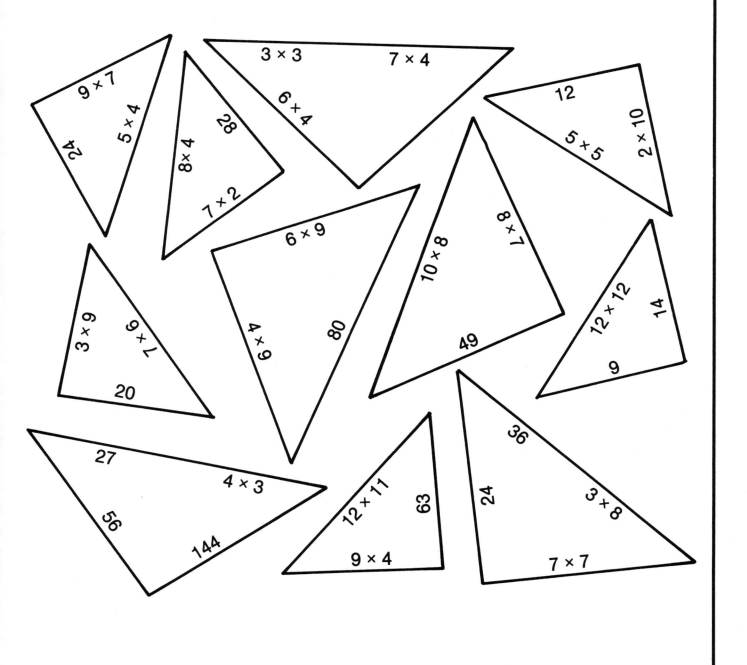

GA279

A NUMBER OF SHAPES INDEPENDENT STUDY CARDS

How many rectangles can you find in the drawing below?

How many triangles can you find in the triangle below?

How many triangles can you find in the shape below?

How many squares can you find in the drawing below?

GA279

BRAVO for you!

_____. I know now I can always count on you to do what you say you'll do.

_____
(teacher)

_____

wins the **OLLIE OWL AWARD** for wise work in math.

_____
(teacher)

GA279

MEASUREMENT CENTER

It is convenient if you can place this center near a sink. Students will then have a better chance to compare various liquid measures. If this is impossible, obtain a large quantity of beans, unpopped popcorn, or other small pelleted objects that can be used to compare the containers or vessels which hold various amounts of liquid measure. Things to put in your measurement center include

metersticks	scales
yardsticks	clocks
tape measures	thermometers
rulers	gallon containers
measuring cups	graph paper
measuring spoons	pencils
liter containers	felt-tipped markers
quart containers	calipers
pint containers	protractors
weights	

GA279

MEASURES OF PURCHASE

In what quantity do we buy each of the following?

milk _____   gallon

bacon _____   pound

gasoline _____   dozen

butter _____   box

rolls _____   ounce

eggs _____   bar

cereal _____   carton

hamburger _____   can

orange juice _____ roll

beans _____   loaf

soap _____   sack

soda pop _____   quart

soup _____   cake

chili _____

steak _____

hot dogs _____

tissue _____

buns _____

candy _____

gum _____

GA279

THERMOMETRY

Water freezes at 32⁰ Fahrenheit and boils at 212⁰ Fahrenheit. Show both of the extremes in the thermometers to the right.

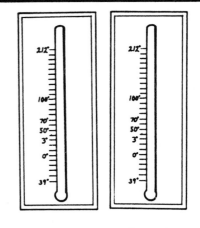

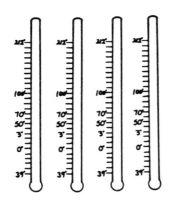

Show the following temperatures in the thermometers to the left by shading in the correct levels: 40⁰, 72⁰, 93⁰, 16⁰

Show a thermometer that registers 12⁰ below freezing, then one that registers 12⁰ above freezing.

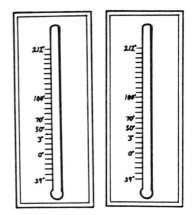

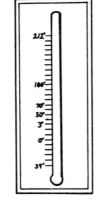

Show a thermometer that is exactly 19⁰ below the boiling point of water.

Find out about the *normal body temperature* and show that temperature on the thermometer to the left. How does a person feel when his or her body temperature rises above this mark?

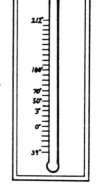

Show a temperature you think would be correct for a "very hot summer day."

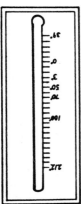

Shade in the way you like the "mercury" to register when you are *most* comfortable.

GA279

The Celsius thermometer shows 0⁰ to be the freezing point and 100⁰ to be the boiling point of water.

These days many of those bank thermometers which alternate between flashing the time and the temperature are also including a Celsius reading. Look at the comparisons to the right.

In each case both the Fahrenheit reading and the Celsius thermometer are saying the same thing. They're just saying it in different ways.

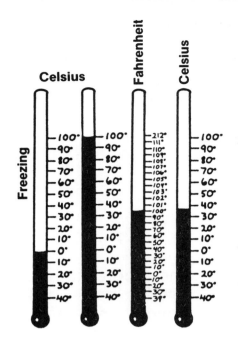

To change a Fahrenheit reading to a Celsius reading, you need to subtract 32⁰ from the Fahrenheit scale first and then multiply the result by 5/9. Try one of the above just to see if it works.

On the other hand, if you want to change a Celsius reading to the Fahrenheit scale, you need to multiply the Celsius reading by 9/5 first, then add 32 to the product. Try the other comparison above to see if you are doing the work correctly.

Below are some thermometers which show either Fahrenheit readings or Celsius readings. In the blank thermometer write in the correct reading that is missing after you have made your calculations and shaded in the area.

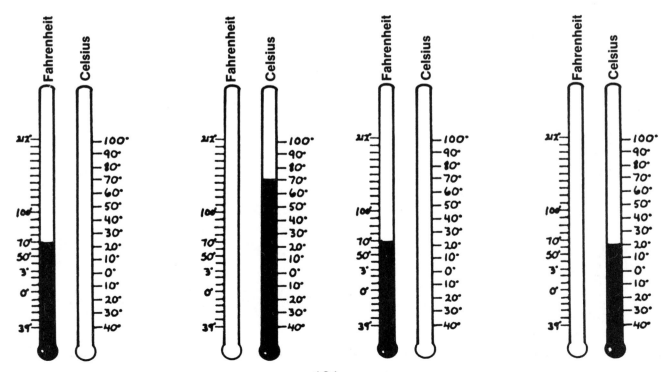

101

AN "AVERAGE" DAY

The high temperature for November 3 was 72⁰ Fahrenheit, while the low for that day was 46⁰ Fahrenheit. What was the difference in degrees between the high and the low on that particular day?

The record high for the day (November 3) was 81⁰ set back in 1946. The record low for a November 3 was 24⁰ Fahrenheit recorded in 1928. What is the difference in degrees between the record high and record low temperatures for November 3?

On this November 3, was the high (72⁰) or the low (46⁰) closer to the daily records for this day?

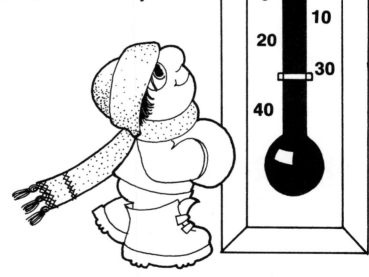

The average high and low temperatures for this day are 63⁰ for a high average and 36⁰ for an average low reading. Would you say that this particular November 3 was "above average" or "below average"? How did you arrive at this decision?

GA279

Let's do a little research on your own. When you get up in the morning look at your thermometer at home. Record that temperature. Look at it again just before you come to school. Then, just as soon as you get home from school, look again. Record the temperature a fourth time right after you eat dinner and record a final reading just before you go to bed.

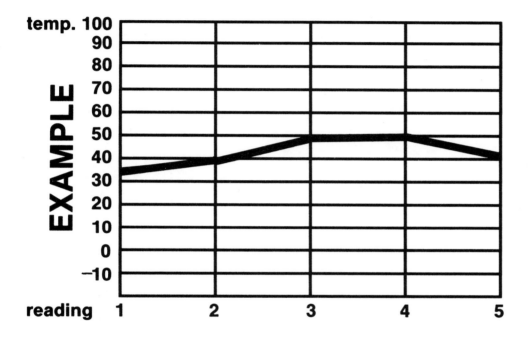

What time of day was the temperature the lowest?

At what time of day was it the highest?

Would you say that the day was "average," "above average" or "below average"?

Find in another source (radio, TV or the newspaper) the record high and low temperatures for the day. Then put all this information together (plus any other neat "weather facts" you can think of) and prepare a short report to hand in to your teacher.

GA279

METRIC MYSTERIES

Unscramble these metric terms so that they are arranged from the smallest to the largest. Place the largest in the box on top and the smallest unit prefix on the bottom.

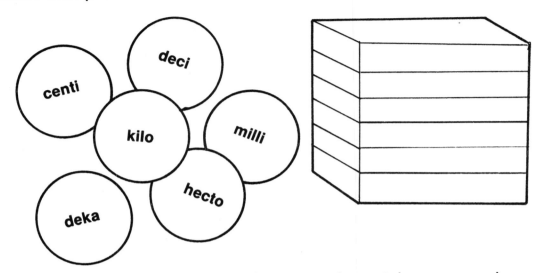

Match the units in each case that are closest by comparison. Draw connecting lines to show relationship between units.

pound	**meter**
inch	**kilogram**
quart	**centimeter**
yard	**gram**
mile	**kilometer**
ounce	**liter**

Which of the metric units on this page would be appropriate for measuring each of the following?

The weight of a catfish _____

The length of a football field _____

The height of the basket in the gym _____

The amount of water in the swimming pool _____

The capacity of a car's gas tank _____

The weight of a hamburger _____

The distance from your house to school _____

The weight of a ladybug _____

The length of your thumb _____

GA27

When students are out of your room, measure with a metric stick the length of several objects in your classroom. Then post the measurements of those objects on the bulletin board. Do not in any way reveal the identity of the objects you measured. Divide students into teams with each team being given a metric stick. Their team task is to discover those objects which you measured.

Be very precise in the accuracy of your measurements. Your students will be very upset if they measure something that you've measured and get a different answer.

GA279

MAIN STREET MATH
A REAL BUY!

When surveyors measured the Northwest Territory following the Land Ordinance of 1787, it was decided that the land would be offered for sale to the general public and that records of the transactions would be officially kept to avoid possible further conflicts over land ownership as well as preventing "claim-jumping" practices of the past.

The land was sold in parcels that were all based on this single standard:

> ## 1 SECTION = 640 ACRES

What measure are you familiar with that contains 640 acres?

Even if a man did have enough money to buy a whole section of land, he didn't have the farm machinery nor the modern technology that was needed to maintain such a large farm. So. . .land was sold in half-section tracts. How many acres were there in a half-section?

1 half section	**1 half section**

**1 SECTION
640 ACRES**

GA279

Land was also sold in quarter-sections. How many acres were there in a quarter-section of land?

A smaller farmer could buy a half-quarter section. How many acres were there in a half-quarter section?

He could even buy a quarter-quarter section, in which case he would have purchased how many acres of land?

Some of this land sold for as little as $1.25/acre. How much would a farmer have had to pay for each of these land parcels?

Whole Section $_____

Half-Section $_____

Quarter-Section $_____

Half-Quarter Section $_____

Quarter-Quarter Section $_____

	half-quarter section	quarter-section
quarter-quarter section		half-section
	WHOLE SECTION	

GA279

That same land today is worth many times what it cost back in 1790. In fact much of that very land is worth as much as $4000/acre. Considering today's prices, what would a half-section of land be worth today?

How about a quarter-quarter section?

A half-quarter section?

A whole section?

AND FOR THOSE BEYOND. . . .

What percentage of an increase would exist if someone had bought some land way back then and passed it on to his heirs. . .who in turn passed it on to their heirs. . etc. . .the land being handed down from one generation to the next. . .with the same parcel of land remaining "in the family"? The family who owned it today would have an increased investment of what percent over the original investment?

And just suppose. . .that all of Illinois was for sale. What would it have been worth in 1790?
What would it be worth today?

GA27

WHICH IS THE. . . ?

Show your tremendous knowledge of the relationship that exists between the various standards of weights and measures. Circle your responses.

Which is *longest*?
1 mile   1 kilometer   5200 feet

Which is *longest*?
2 meters   2.5 yards   84 inches

Which is *heaviest*?
2600 pounds   2 tons   2500 kilograms

Which is *longest*?
440 yards   400 meters   1/8 mile

Which weighs the *least*?
.5 pounds   10 ounces   27 grams

Which is *longest*?
2 millimeters   2 centimeters   2 inches

Which is the *most* money?
23 dimes   9 quarters   41 nickels

Which is the *latest*?
9:50 p.m.   11:30 a.m.   noon

Which of these temperatures is the *warmest*?
10ºC   -10ºF   30ºF

Which is the *most*?
2 liters   1/2 gallon   9 pints

Which is the *least*?
14 cups   1 gallon   1.5 liters

Which is the *least* amount of $$$$?
56 nickels $5 bill   17 quarters

GA279

MAIN STREET MATH
CHANGING TIMES

Look closely at the various time zones that cover the continental United States. Then find a map that locates its major cities. Using the map below, add or subtract hours to get the correct answer in each case.

1. If it is 3:00 a.m. in Chicago, Illinois, what time is it in New York City?

   _____

2. If it is 2:00 p.m. in Miami, Florida, what time is it in Kansas City, Missouri?

   _____

3. What time is it in Los Angeles when it is 4:30 a.m. in Atlanta, Georgia?

   _____

4. What time is it in Salt Lake City, Utah, when it's 11:30 a.m. in New Orleans, Louisiana?

   _____

5. What time is it in Columbus, Ohio, when it is 11:45 p.m. in Duluth, Minnesota?

   _____

6. If it is noon in our nation's capital, what time is it in Houston, Texas?

   _____

7. What time is it in New York City when it is 2:25 a.m. in Denver, Colorado?

   _____

8. What time is it in Boston, Massachusetts, when it's 2:45 a.m. in Birmingham, Alabama?

   _____

9. If it's 3:45 p.m. in Dallas, Texas, what time is it in Las Vegas, Nevada?

   _____

10. What time is it in San Francisco when it's 7:30 a.m. in Tulsa, Oklahoma?

   _____

GA27

11. If it is 11:40 a.m. in Seattle, Washington, what time is it in Tampa, Florida?

_____

12. If it is 3:10 a.m. in Pittsburgh, Pennsylvania, what time is it in Salem, Oregon?

_____

13. What time is it in Tucson, Arizona, when it is 8:15 a.m. in St. Louis, Missouri?

_____

14. If you lived in Los Angeles and wanted to call your friend in Boston to wish her a "Happy New Year" precisely at 12:00 midnight in Boston, what time should you place your call?

_____

15. If it is 3:00 p.m. in Lansing, Michigan, what time is it in San Antonio, Texas?

_____

16. If it is 9:35 p.m. in New Orleans, what time is it in Seattle?

_____

17. What time is it in Minneapolis if it is 8:18 a.m. in Phoenix?

_____

18. If it is 5:00 in the morning in Tampa, what time is it in San Diego?

_____

19. If it is 9:00 a.m. in Raleigh, what time is it where you live?

_____

20. A plane leaves from Phoenix at 1:30 p.m. and is in flight for two and one-half hours. If that plane lands in Nashville, Tennessee, at what time should the passengers set their watches if they want to have the correct time?

_____

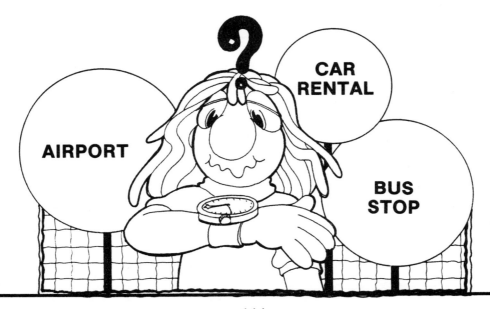

AIRPORT

CAR RENTAL

BUS STOP

GA279

AS THE CROW FLIES

Locate these major U.S. cities on the map below. Then calculate the air distance in miles between the cities in the problems below (using the scale of miles). Place your answer in the blank space provided.

⊢——⊣ = 200 miles

1. Chicago to New York _____
2. Los Angeles to Denver _____
3. Dallas to St. Louis _____
4. Washington D.C., to New Orleans _____
5. Kansas City to Boston _____
6. Atlanta to Minneapolis _____
7. Seattle to Miami _____
8. Portland to San Francisco _____
9. Philadelphia to Houston _____
10. Tampa to San Diego _____
11. Buffalo to Birmingham _____
12. Nashville to Phoenix _____
13. Tucson to Pittsburgh _____
14. Las Vegas to Cleveland _____

GA27

First estimate, then measure and finally record your comparisons for the following:

Estimate	Units	Actual	Units
diagonal of your TV set			
height of a bicycle			
perimeter of the school			
weight of your pencil			

First estimate, then measure and finally record your comparisons for the following:

Estimate	Units	Actual	Units
length of your bed			
length of your tooth-brush			
distance across your plate			
perimeter of your house			

First estimate, then measure and finally record your comparisons for the following:

Estimate	Units	Actual	Units
the length of your shoe			
the depth of the waste basket			
your teacher's height			
the distance from your desk to the door			
Distance across the foot-ball field			

First estimate, then measure and finally record your comparisons for the following:

Estimate	Units	Actual	Units
the length of your pencil			
the width of your math book			
the height of a 16-oz. pop bottle			
the distance around a tree			

GA279

_____
(student)

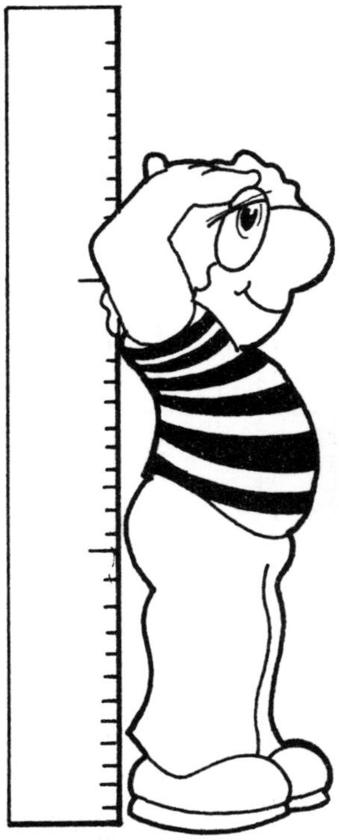

You've Really Measured Up in Math

_____
(from)

_____
(student)

was with us every inch of the way

_____
(from)

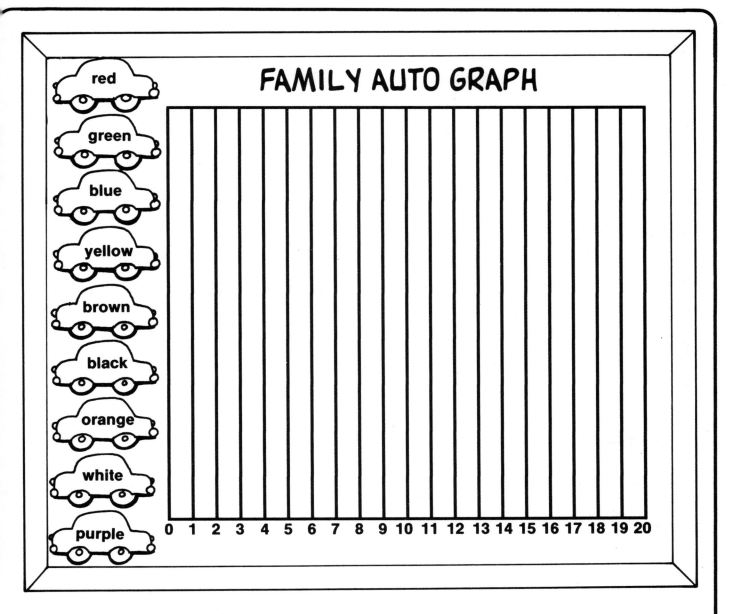

Here's a bulletin board idea that is useful in introducing students to the skill of charting and graphing. The background is made from some light colored construction paper or oak tag. Create the actual grid for recording information from a darker more contrasting colored paper. Cut out shapes of cards from construction paper. Letters for the title should be made from colorful paper.

You are now ready to "poll" your class on the various colors of cars they have in their families. It is appropriate to first create a simple distribution chart on the chalkboard for the various colors before placing the compiled information on the bar graph. Once all the information has been gathered, ask different students to go to the bulletin board and fill in the appropriate line length according to the information he or she has. It will look neater if you use black construction paper for the bar, but a black felt-tipped marker will be much easier.

GRAPHING/STATISTICS/PROBABILITY CENTER

WORK SHEETS

If children are not very familiar with the independence that accompanies learning center/contract type of work, they often tend to develop some rather questionable study habits. In fact, some actually reach the point where they regard time spent in the learning center as merely free time or fun time.

To help overcome such an atmosphere the teacher should first spend enough class time to explain fully just what is expected, both in terms of accomplishment and also behavior.

Attractive bulletin boards also help to spark the interest of young minds in the presentation of certain material. It might also prove beneficial to place a related bulletin board message near the learning center itself to provide further stimulation.

116

THEIR FAVORITE FOOD

One day during recess several of the students in Miss Robinson's 5th grade class somehow got on the subject of favorite foods. Todd, Teri Ann and Wendy all insisted that pizza was the greatest, while Randy, Tami and Chad were just as certain that a burger and fries had them all beat! Tommy then chimed in that they were all crazy and "everyone who knows anything knows that steak is best!"

Miss Robinson overheard this little conversation and decided to step in before the discussion went any further. "Rather than just stand here and argue about it, let's ask all the kids in the fifth grade. This still won't change any of your minds, nor will it prove anything about which food really *is* best; but it might be fun to find out for your own information about the tastes of our fifth grade students."

Since the children all agreed, Miss Robinson gave them instructions on how to conduct a *survey*. A *survey* is really a gathering of the opinions of people concerning a topic (like "favorite food"). You can ask all of the people in a particular group (like the whole 4th grade) . . .or you may be able to get a pretty good idea of their choices simply by asking a few.

For example, if you wanted to ask the question, "What is the favorite food of 5th graders in America?" you wouldn't have to ask *every* 5th grade kid in the United States. You could take samples of opinions of kids from various parts of the country and you would have a pretty good idea of their choice.

Once you have all of this information, you need to put it down on paper so that it will be meaningful to others. There are a number of ways you can show this. One of the ways is through the use of a *bar graph*.

On the next page you will see the results of the survey of Miss Robinson's class. There are eight sections of the fifth grade in Washington Elementary School. The average class size is from 23-26 students per class.

FAVORITE FOOD

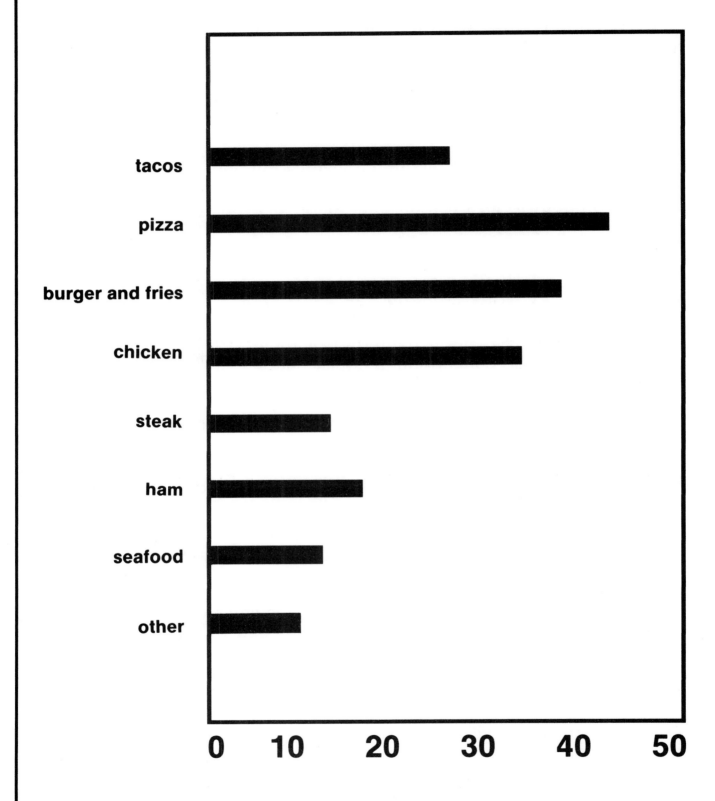

GA279

How many kids were polled in this little *survey*?

If there are 204 kids in the 5th grade at Washington Elementary, why weren't 204 kids *surveyed*?

What conclusions can you draw from the results of this little survey?

What was the favorite food of 5th graders at Washington Elementary?

What do you suppose some of those "other" favorite foods included?

Do you think these results would be the same if the poll were to be conducted nationally?

Conduct your own *survey* just like the kids in Miss Robinson's class did. You can survey just the members of your class. . .or you can get some friends to help and survey the whole grade you are in. . . or you can become really ambitious and survey the entire school (if it isn't too big). Just be sure to follow the same steps Miss Robinson's class used. When you're finished, place your findings on a bar graph similar to the one they used.

What are some other reasons for people conducting *surveys*?

GA279

SCALING, SCALING . . .

If your teacher asked you to make a drawing of your desk and all of the things that are in it, you'd probably look inside first to see just how your books, papers and other school supplies are arranged. Then you would probably attempt to make a drawing that looked somewhat like that arrangement. But how really *accurate* would your drawing be? First, would your math book be the same size in your drawing as it really is when compared to the area it occupies in your desk? Probably not!

To make your drawing more accurate, you can use a *grid* like the one on this page. Your teacher may have some graph paper, or you can even make your own. Use a ruler to measure and let each box represent one inch in real length of your desk. Then mark off those areas that are occupied by the various things in your desk and your drawing should be much more accurate than it was the first time.

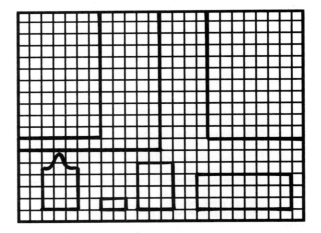

Once you've finished this, make a scale drawing of your locker and its contents. Don't forget to measure. This time you may have to let the length of one of those little boxes represent two or even three inches. Remember to be consistent throughout your measurements.

GA27

How about making a *scale drawing* of your room at home. Again, be sure to change your *scale* or you won't be able to get the whole drawing on a single sheet of paper.

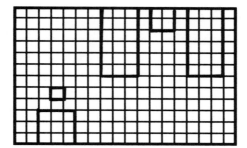

A good class project would be to create a *scale drawing* of your entire classroom. . .then maybe even the WHOLE SCHOOL!

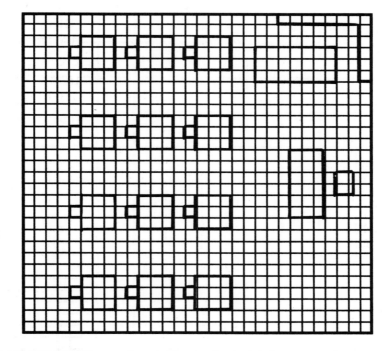

A REALLY AMBITIOUS project that should be worth extra credit would be to make a scale drawing of the whole block on which you live. Be sure to include all the buildings and houses and other things that occupy space.

So you're saying by now, "what's next, the whole town? Then what. . . the entire state?. . .all of America. . .the whole world?" No, we won't ask that of you, but are you starting to get the idea of how people who make maps go about doing their work?

GA279

CHARTING PORKY

The nose begins at (6, 21), then extends to (8, 21). Continuing in a clockwise fashion, write complete instructions for the location of the coordinates that will complete the pig in the drawing below.

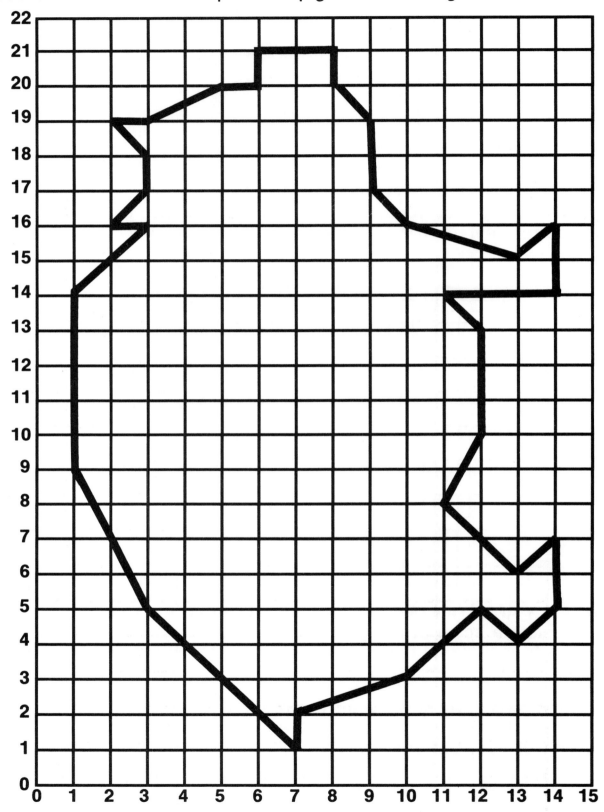

Create your own animal by connecting lines between these coordinates. The first dot is already in place for you at (3,22). Your task is to complete the rest of the drawing. (4,22) (5,21) (5,16) (4,15) (7,15) (10,18) (12,18) (13,18) (13,15) (12,14) (11,14) (10,15) (9,15) (9,14) (10,13) (10,12) (8,10) (8,9) (11,6) (11,4) (12,5) (13,5) (14,4) (14,3) (13,2) (12,2) (11,3) (10,2)) (7,2) (6,3) (5,2) (2,2) (2,3) (3,3) (3,8) (4,9) (4,10) (2,12) (2,13) (3,14) (3,15) (2,16) (2,21)

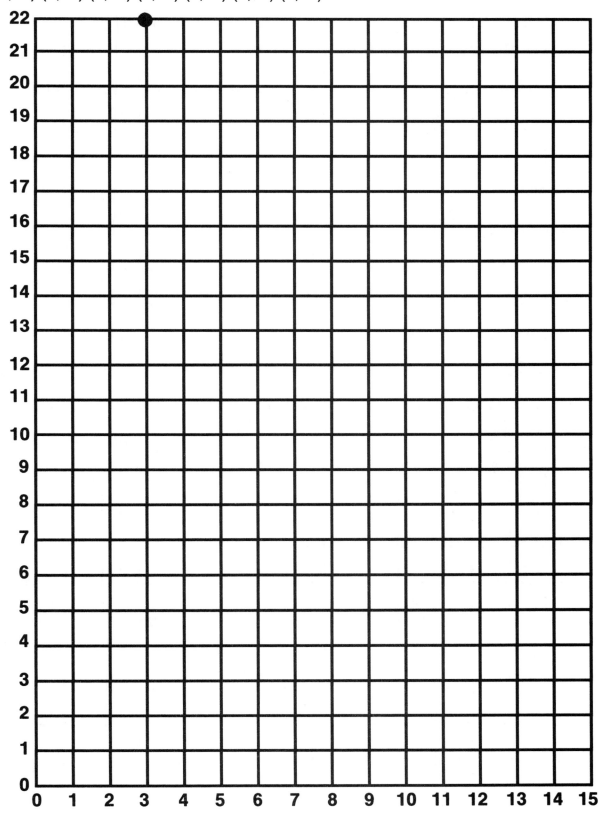

HOP-A-LONG COORDINATES

MAIN STREET MATH
THEIR FAVORITE COLOR

Have you ever had anybody ask you the burning question, "What's your favorite color?" I bet you have one, too. Is it blue (a popular one)?. . .or red?. . .or green?. . .or perhaps black?

Have you ever wondered what is the most popular choice of "favorite color"? Well, one way to find out would be to just go up and ask people, "Hey, you, what's your favorite color?" If that sounds crazy, maybe there's another way.

Lots of times people get up in the morning and, without even thinking, choose a shirt or top from the closet that is their favorite color. If we think this is true, then we won't even have to ask people. We'll just look at what a whole bunch of people are wearing.

To help you with this little *survey*, pick a friend who can serve as your aid in *counting* and marking.

Set up several columns on a sheet of paper to *tally* the different colors of tops.

Choose a nice warm day when people won't be wearing coats (to cover up their shirts).

Pick a busy street corner (or maybe the edge of the school grounds) or some place where you know people will be walking past.

GA27

As each person goes by, you or your friend should make a mark on your sheet in the right column. You could separate males from females, but that might get you all fouled up. You can try that next time.

You'll have to stay there more than just a few minutes, because to conduct a really good survey you need a large *sample*.

When you think you can't stand doing surveys any longer, go home armed with your *data* and figure out what you've got.

Count the tally marks. What color was #1? Which choice was the second most popular, etc.?

Can you say with certainty now that "More people like blue tops (or whatever choice was #1) than any other"?

What are some things that might have made your survey invalid? What if several people chose another shirt because their favorite was dirty. . .or in the clothes dryer. . .or was torn?

For those of you who are really into *statistics*, change your results to percentages (like they do on TV when they say "57 percent of the dentists surveyed chose Crest").

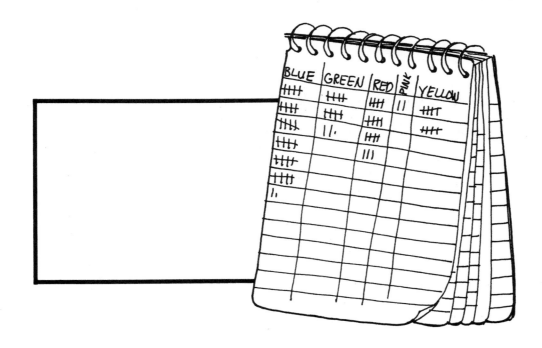

GA279

STATUS

The word has a certain magic ring to it in our society. It really means a lot of things. . .the kind of house you live in, the kind of car you drive, how much education you have, the clothes you wear, the company you keep. . .and more. . .much more. But the bottom line usually boils down to money—"How much does it cost?"

Look at each of the groups of "similars" below and on the next page and decide which in each group has the *greatest status* (based on the simple fact that it costs the most). Place the number 1 beside that choice; then a 2 beside the second choice of the status seeker, etc. Continue this rating all the way through the number 5, which would be the last choice of the status seeker. If you are unfamiliar with the actual dollar figure that should be associated with each, you may have to do a little checking around. Ask your parents or teacher for help.

When you're all done with your rating, look back and try to decide which of these categories is *most important* to you at this point.

Which status do you think is *most important* to most adults?

TRANSPORTATION:

_____ Cadillac

_____ Toyota

_____ Monte Carlo

_____ Buick Electra

_____ Mercedes Benz

EDUCATION:

_____ Master's Degree

_____ High School Diploma

_____ Doctorate

_____ Junior High Diploma

_____ Bachelor of Arts Degree

OCCUPATIONS:

_____ Brain Surgeon

_____ Sanitation Engineer

_____ Factory Worker

_____ Teacher

_____ Truck Driver

GA2790

SHELTERS:

_____ Ocean-front Con-
         dominium

_____ Split Level

_____ Colonial Mansion

_____ Government Housing
         Project

_____ Apartment

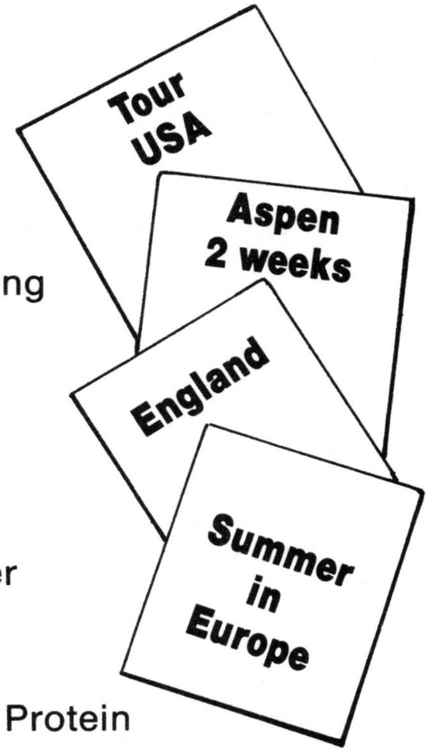

CLOTHING:

_____ Botany 500

_____ Made in Taiwan

_____ Sears

_____ Cricketeer

_____ Neiman-Marcus

FOODS:

_____ Lobster

_____ Hamburger

_____ Roast

_____ Steak

_____ Vegetable Protein
         Meat

VACATIONS:

_____ Long Weekend

_____ Two-Month Tour of
         USA

_____ Two Weeks at Aspen

_____ One Week in New
         England

_____ Summer in Europe

Tour USA

Aspen 2 weeks

England

Summer in Europe

What other status symbols can you think of?

_____

_____

_____

What makes them so?

_____

_____

_____

_____

GA279

THE OTHER SIDE OF THE COIN

You've seen the two captains of football teams meeting in the center of the field with the officials before the game for the traditional toss of the coin, which determines who gets the ball first, which team "gets the wind" and which team gets its choice of goals.

Have you ever wondered how the captain decides whether to call "heads" or "tails"? Is heads really any better than tails? What if he called "heads" last time and won? Should he stick with heads. . .or should he switch to tails? What should he choose if he lost the flip before the last game by choosing "heads"?

If a captain called "heads" every time, how many times would you expect him to win the flip this season if his team plays ten games?

Try it yourself. Toss the coin ten times and record the number of times you get heads and the number of times you get tails.

Try this experiment a second time. Did you get the same number of heads? Try the experiment again a third time. Can you come to any conclusions about this little experiment?

_____
_____
_____
_____
_____
_____
_____
_____
_____
_____
_____
_____

GA279

What kind of result would you expect if you flipped the coin 100 times? Find a friend to help and try it!

What if you had two coins and flipped them both? Let's say you have a quarter and a dime. If you flip them both, what are the *odds* that they will both come up heads?

Look at the possible combinations:

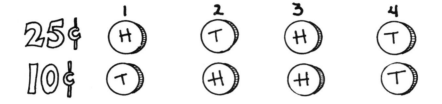

Using the above information, if you flipped both coins 20 times, how many times would you expect the flip to result in both coins turning up heads?

How did you arrive at this "theory"?

_____

_____

_____

_____

_____

_____

Get a friend to help and try it.

GA279

MAIN STREET MATH
COUNT ME IN!

Below are some population figures of Calvin County. They represent a comparison of the 1980 census with the census taken in 1990.

Do you know what the word *census* means? Look it up in the dictionary if you don't know. Jot down a definition of the word *census*.

_____

_____

_____

Every ten years the government conducts a head count of all the people in the United States.

So you wonder why the government spends millions of dollars just to find out how many people there are in the United States. Good question. There are really some pretty good reasons for doing this. Among them is to decide how much money each city gets to help provide the governmental services for the people who live there.

Your next question is probably, "What are *governmental services*?" Ask your teacher. Discuss *governmental services* in class.

What are some other reasons for the government wanting to know how many people there are and where they all live?

City	1990	1980
Hoopston	728	734
Johnson City	1391	1297
Harmony	479	576
Pilot Grove	1131	1047
Wilcox	1840	1748
Bowen	522	489
Browning	1819	1701
Rockport	1261	1036
Montebello	4138	3379
Rocky Creek	527	610
Carthage	2970	3350
Sonora	616	576
Warsaw	1406	1284
Pontoosuc Village	261	226

GA279

1. What was the total population of Calvin County in 1990?

   _____

2. How does that figure compare with the population of Calvin County in 1980?

   _____

3. Which towns have increased in population?

   _____
   _____
   _____
   _____
   _____   _____
   _____   _____
   _____   _____

4. Which have decreased (gone down) in population? _____
   _____
   _____

5. Which city had the most people in 1980? _____

6. Which city is the largest now? _____

7. Which city has gone down the most in population? _____

8. What does all this mean to the residents of Calvin County? _____
   _____
   _____
   _____

9. List some of the kinds of *governmental services* that are supported by our tax dollars.

   _____
   _____
   _____
   _____

GA279

A WELL-ROUNDED DAY. . .

Have you ever sat down and really thought about how much of your day you spend eating. . .and sleeping. . .and watching TV. . .and even studying?

We can let a circle stand for a whole 24-hour day (and night). Then we can mark off the sections of that circle (much like cutting a pie) that stand for how much of each day we spend doing different things. For example, if you spent 12 hours eating and 12 hours sleeping, your graph might look like this:

But we all know this just isn't true. We do lots of other things during each day, too. Look at how this next little gentleman impressed his math teacher by showing "graphically" how he spent his day.

GA279

To picture your own day, get a 12-inch pizza wheel cut from tagboard from your teacher. Then do the following:

1. Keep track of the approximate amount of time you spend doing different things in the next 24 hours.

2. To make it easier (and so you won't have to try to remember), write down the times.

3. Then add the totals in each category (eating, sleeping, watching TV, etc.).

4. Change each total to a fraction with a denominator of 24 (since that's how many hours there are in a day) and then reduce the fraction to its lowest terms. For example, if you slept 8 hours, your fraction would be 8/24 = 1/3.

5. Mark off the various "pieces" of your pie on the circle and label them. In the example above, 1/3 of the circle should be marked off and labeled "sleeping."

12-inch tagboard pizza wheel

sleeping

GA279

MAIN STREET MATH
HOW DOES YOUR GARDEN GROW?

When Tammy and Chad asked their father if they could help with the family garden, he told them, "I'll do more than that. I'll give you two an entire section of the garden. You can plan the whole thing. I'll even buy the seed. Then you can set up a stand and sell what you produce and keep the money."

Well, you certainly can't beat a deal like that! So, Tammy and Chad began looking through the seed catalog. They decided to "weed out" several of the offerings and choose from the following vegetables: tomatoes, green beans, peas, sweet corn, radishes and onions. The burning question was. . .How much of each?

You see a scale drawing on the next page of the plot their father had given to them.

Below you see portions of the labels.

PEAS - Plant in double rows 3 inches apart, spacing seeds 2 inches apart. One pkt. contains 225 seeds and will plant a 25-ft. row. One pkt. costs $ .80.

TOMATOES - Start seeds in individual pots indoors 6-8 weeks before planting. Stake plants 2 feet apart in rows 3 feet apart. There are 30 seeds in each pkt. which sells for $ .95.

GREEN BEANS - Plant in rows 24 inches apart. Make furrows 2 inches deep and space beans 3 inches apart. There are about 200 seeds in each package. One pkt. costs $ .85.

ONION SETS - Plant in rows 2 feet apart, spacing sets 3 inches apart. One pound will plant a 50-ft. row. The sets cost $2.75 per half-pound.

SWEET CORN - Plant in rows 3 feet apart, spacing the seeds 6 inches apart. Later thin to stand 12 inches apart. One pkt. contains approximately 200 seeds.

GA279

Decide with a friend the layout you would suggest to Tammy and Chad. Prepare a drawing that will show your final decisions on *what* you want to plant, on *how much* you want to buy and on *where* you want to plant each of the vegetables.

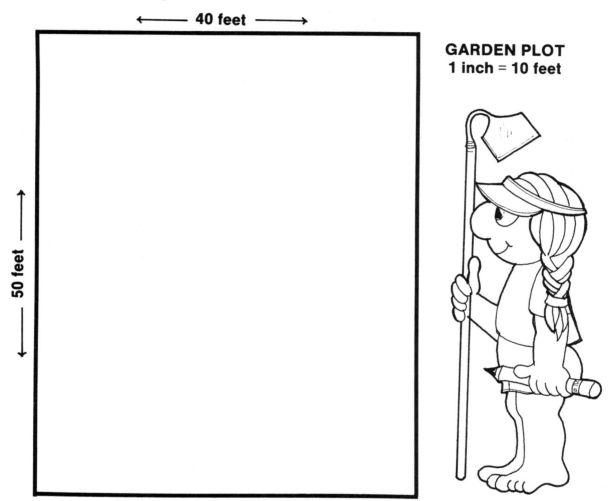

← 40 feet →

50 feet

GARDEN PLOT
1 inch = 10 feet

When you have finished planning your garden, figure out how much money they should charge for each item at their "roadside stand" in order to make money.

To do this you'll no doubt need to check in some grocery stores to see what they charge. Then you will probably want to advise them to charge just a little bit less.

Why should they do this?

If you do your checking in the middle of winter, why won't this give you a very good idea of what you should tell these kids to charge?

To estimate just how much Tammy and Chad are going to make this summer, what other facts would you need to know?

GA279

COORDINATE TIC-TAC

Construct game boards from tagboard similar to the board shown below. Draw a grid with black felt-tipped marker and cover with Con-Tact paper to ensure durability. Also needed is a pair of dice plus several small tokens (coins, grains, etc.).

To play this game all players first roll the dice. The highest roller plays first. He rolls each die separately. The first roll is charted on the vertical scale and the second roll is charted on the horizontal scale. At the intersection of the two, the player should place one of the tokens. Play then passes on to the next player.

The first player to chart a line of six tokens in a row (either vertically, horizontally or diagonally) wins the game.

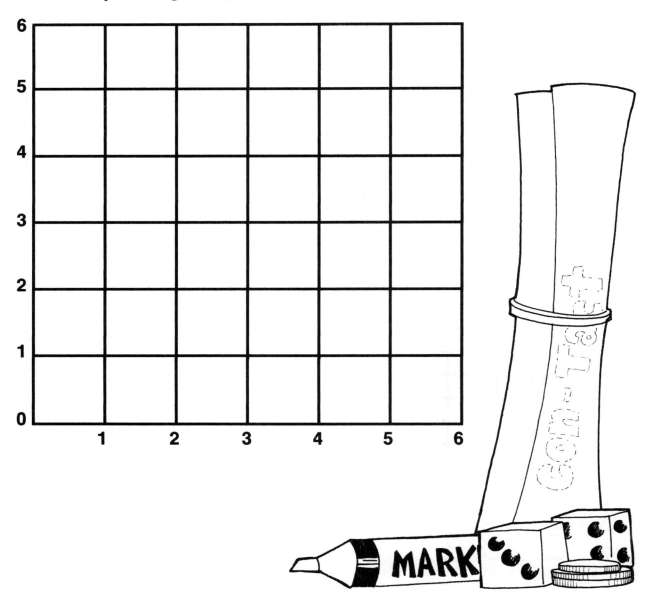

GA27

Construct a graph on the color of eyes of all the students in your class.

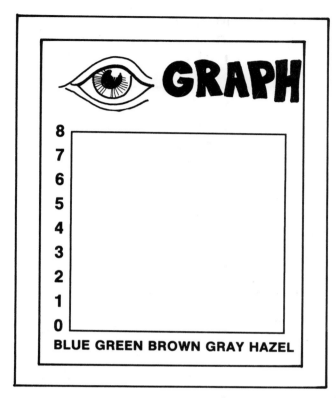

Graph the length of your various body parts in centimeters.

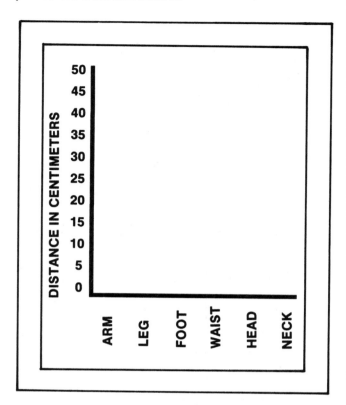

Chart the number of birthdays each month holds for the students in your class.

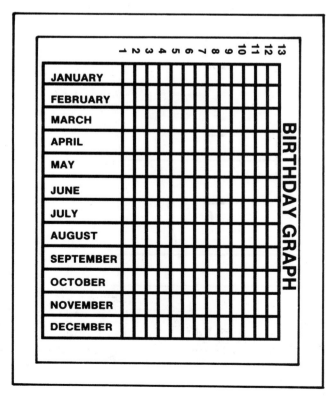

Survey 24 people who are not in your class on their favorite pet. Record their response on the chart below.

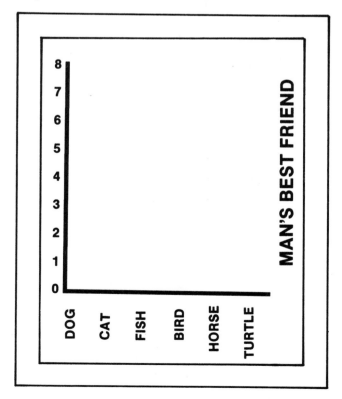

137

GA279

CONGRATULATIONS

_____

YOU'VE REACHED THE TOP!

_____
(teacher)

YOU'RE A-O.K.!

_____

GOOD WORK!

_____
(teacher)

_____

_____

_____

GA279

ANSWER KEY

. . .And When In Rome. . . Page 12

LXXXVIII = 88	386 = CCCLXXXI
CMXC = 990	999 = IM
MCMXVI = 1916	62 = LXII
KLVII = 47	18 = XVIII
CMXLI = 941	436 = CDXXXVI
DCCXLVII = 747	706 = DCCVI
MCMLXIV = 1964	1012 = MXII
	1981 = CMLXXXI
	2482 = MMLXXXII

Pink Pony Cafe Page 14

41,876; 42,203 Last year was < than year ago; 32,718, 30,969; 5232 2 years ago, 4848 last year

Pink Pony Cafe (cont'd.) Page 15

4615, 4816, customers were thirstier two years ago
3826 2 years ago, 4088 last year

Good. . .Better. . .Best. . . Page 24

A 96-oz. bottle of fabric softener for $5.19 is the best buy

Good. . .Better. . .Best. . . (cont'd.) Page 25

A small 12-inch pizza for $5.95
one-pound box (16-oz.) of breakfast food for $1.99
two cassettes for $14.95
six breakfast rolls for $.89
three ties for $16.00
one dozen of the same balls for $22.00
three heads for $1.77
four colored pens for $.99
Brand names, quantity needed, desired

Number Worms Page 28

$3 + 4 - 5 + 6 = 8$
$1 + 2 + 3 - 4 = 2$
$6 - 5 + 3 + 2 = 6$
$2 + 9 - 5 - 3 = 3$
$6 - 4 + 1 + 4 = 7$
$3 - 2 + 4 - 1 = 4$

Let the Sum Shine In Page 31

1352

Oscar N. Octopus Page 34

62; 137; 77; 8; 1; 2; 22; 33; 27; 369

More Number Worms Page 35

$6 \times 3 = 18 \div 12 = 1.5 \times 8 = 12$
$3 \times 2 = 6 \times 8 = 48 \div 3 = 16$
$10 - 5 = 5 \times 12 = 60 \div 20 = 3 \div 3 = 1$
$3 + 8 = 11 + 4 = 15 \times 6 = 90 \div 30 = 3$
$21 - 3 = 18 \div 3 = 6 \times 14 = 84 \div 21 = 4$

Balancing Box Page 40

$13 + 8 + 17$
$12 + 10 + 16$
$18 + 5 + 15$
$4 + 32 + 2$
$3 + 21 + 14$

Group of Animals Study Cards Page 41

Troup of kangaroos, Rafter of turkeys, Gaggle of Geese, Parliament of owls

Magic Squares Page 48

2	8	16
8	4	2
16	2	32

5	5	25
1	15	15
5	75	375

6	3	18
2	1	2
3	3	9

81	2	162
3	1	3
27	2	54

3	2	6
3	3	1
1	6	6

Mileage Math Page 52

$25.08, 25.5 miles per gallon, 4.47 cents per mile

Classified Math Page 60

$57.60, $120, $10 per month; $6.75, $.75; $60; $510.50, $90

Anatomy of the Electricity Bill Page 63

1. $1691.41
2. 29,916 kwh
3. 368
4. It depends on when the meter was read each month. Twelve readings could exceed 365 if the meter reader was not there the same day each month.
5. $140.95 average
6. $4.60
7. February 4023
8. February
9. Power companies oftentimes have higher rates during summer months.
10. Answers will vary.
11. Turn off lights when not in use, wash and dry dishes by hand, do not run air conditioner except when necessary, dial thermostat down in winter months when family members go to bed, etc.

Steamboat Pizza Port (cont'd.) Page 66

$70.16

Division Study Cards, Page 68

Chris Evert, Pete Rose, Alberto Salazar, Jack Nicklaus

Sport Shorts Study Cards Page 69

$60 \div 4 = 15 \times 2 = 30 \div 6 = 5 \times 3 = 15 \times 100 = 1500 \div 10 = 150 \times 28 = 4200$
$2 \times 5 = 10 \times 40 = 400 \times 15 = 6000 \div 3 = 2000 \div 10 = 200 \times 4 = 800 \div 5 = 160$
$4 \times 9 = 36 \times 9 = 324 \div 1 = 324 \div 2 = 162 \div 3 = 54 \times 4 = 216 \times 26 = 5616 \times 4 = 22,464 \div 4 = 5616$
$18 \times 1 = 18 \times 5 = 90 \times 2 = 180 \div 3 = 60 \times 14 = 840 \times 72 = 60,480 \div 6 = 10,080 \div 2 = 5040 \div 4 = 1260$

Tracking Fractions Page 73

$6\frac{5}{12}$

GA279

Sunday Afternoon Percentages (cont'd.) Page 79

1. .091
2. .363
3. .182
4. .141
5. .091
6. .454

Sunday Afternoon Percentages (cont'd.) Page 80

7. .464
8. Dallas and Los Angeles
9. Giants have better record than Jets by .727
10. The N.Y. Giants
11. .000

New England, Chicago, Cincinnati, Tampa Bay, Houston, Oakland, Toss up, Minnesota, Kansas City, Giants, Denver, Dallas, Los Angeles

J-Mart Truckload Home Entertainment Sale Page 81

Portable AM/FM Radio $8.91, a savings of $2.97
Portable Color TV $215.91, a savings of $53.97
Stereo $144.00, a savings of $36.00
VCR $263.20, a savings of $65.80
Home Entertainment Center $419.92, a savings of $179.96
Black & White TV $48.92, a savings of $20.96
Traveling Music $112.41, a savings of 37.47
25-inch Console Color TV $299.93, a savings of $199.95

Wheel of Fractions Page 82

7/12, 5/12, Yes

Records of Records Study Cards Page 83

White Christmas, Sound of Music, Elvis Presley, Bing Crosby

A Number of Shapes Page 96

26, 21, 5, 6

Measures of Purchase Page 99

gallon/quart	bar/ounce/quart
pound	ounce
gallon	ounce
pound	ounce/pound/quart
dozen, ounce	pound
dozen	pound
ounce	box
pound/dozen	dozen
ounce	pound/ounce/bar
ounce	ounce

An Average Day Page 102

26°F, 57°, high, above average

Metric Mysteries Page 104

kilo, hecto, deka, deci, centi, milli,
pound-kilogram
inch-centimeter
quart-liter
yard-meter
mile-kilometer
ounce-gram
kilogram, meter, meter, liters, liters, gram, kilometer, gram, centimeter

A Real Buy! Page 106

320 acres

A Real Buy! (cont'd.) Page 107

160 acres, 80, 40, $800, $400, $200, $100, $50

A Real Buy! (cont'd.) Page 108

$1,280,000, $160,000, $320,000, $2,560,000

Which Is the. . . .? Page 109

1 mile, 2.5 yards, 2500 kilograms, 440 yards, 27 grams, 2 inches, 23 dimes, 9:50 p.m., 10°C, 9 pints, 1.5 liters, 56 nickels

Changing Times Page 110

1. 4:00 a.m.
2. 1:00 p.m.
3. 1:30 a.m.
4. 10:30 a.m.
5. 12:45 a.m.
6. 11:00 a.m.
7. 4:25 a.m.
8. 3:45 a.m.
9. 2:45 p.m.
10. 5:30 a.m.

Changing Times Page 111

11. 2:40 p.m.
12. 12:10 a.m.
13. 7:15 a.m.
14. 9:00 p.m.
15. 2:00 p.m.
16. 7:35 p.m.
17. 9:18 a.m.
18. 2:00 a.m.
19. Answers may vary.
20. 5:00 central

As the Crow Flies Page 112

1. 650
2. 700
3. 475
4. 900
5. 1150
6. 825
7. 2575
8. 475
9. 1225
10. 2000
11. 780
12. 1380
13. 1625
14. 1700

Their Favorite Food (cont'd.) Page 119

197
Some may have been absent from school or could not be located when survey was taken.
Pizza was a slight favorite over burger and fries.
Pizza
Answers will vary.
Probably not the same.

Count Me In! Page 131

1. 19,089
2. 1036 more than 1980
3. Johnson City, Pilot Grove, Wilcox, Bowen, Browning, Rockport, Montebello, Sonora, Warsaw, Pontoosuc Village
4. Hoopston, Harmony, Rocky Road, Carthage
5. Montebello
6. Montebello
7. Carthage
8. The county has over 1000 new residents. This means a greater taxing body and thus more money coming in. On the other hand, more people means there should be more people involved in the services provided to the county's residents.

Police and fire protection, libraries, roads and streets, maintenance, health services, welfare services, to name a few.

GA279